WITHDRAWN

BX
4801
.B6

Bowie, Walter
What is Protestantism

BRADNER LIBRARY
SCHOOLCRAFT COLLEGE
LIVONIA, MICHIGAN 48152

WITHDRAWN

What Is Protestantism?

WHAT IS PROTESTANTISM?

Edited by

WALTER RUSSELL BOWIE

and

KENNETH SEEMAN GINIGER

FRANKLIN WATTS, INC.
575 Lexington Avenue, New York, N. Y. 10022

BX
4801
.B6 786w

FIRST PRINTING

Copyright © 1965 by Franklin Watts, Inc.
Library of Congress Catalog Card Number: 65–11755
Printed in the United States of America

Acknowledgments

The editors and publisher herewith render thanks to the following authors, publishers, agents, and copyright owners whose interest, cooperation, and permission to reprint have made possible the publication of this book.

All possible care has been taken to trace the ownership of every selection included and to make full acknowledgment of its use. If any errors have inadvertently occurred, they will be corrected in subsequent editions, provided notification is sent to the publisher.

Abingdon Press for "The Holy Roman Empire" and "John Calvin" from *The Story of the Church* by Walter Russell Bowie. Copyright 1955 by Pierce & Washbaugh. For "Protestant Affirmations" from *A Protestant Manifesto* by Winfred Ernest Garrison. Copyright 1952 by Pierce & Smith. Both by permission of Abingdon Press.

Appleton-Century-Crofts for "Deacon Ballard's Mill" from *George Hodges* by Julia Shelley Hodges. Copyright 1926 by The Century Company. For quotations from the words of Martin Luther from *Martin Luther: The Man and His Work* by Arthur Cushman McGiffert. Reprinted by permission of the publishers Appleton-Century-Crofts, Division of Meredith Publishing Company.

Association Press for the quotation from *Primer for Protestants* by James Hastings Nichols. Copyright 1947 by The Edward W. Hazen Foundation. Permission granted by Association Press.

Brandt & Brandt for quotation from *Western Star* by Stephen Vincent Benét. Published by Holt, Rinehart and Winston, Inc. Copyright 1943 by Rosemary Carr Benét. Reprinted by permission of Brandt & Brandt.

iv

Department of Ministerial Education, Division of Higher Education, Methodist Board of Education for quotations from the words of Martin Luther from "Christian Theology" by Harris Franklin Rall and for "The Genius of Protestantism" by Samuel McCrea Cavert. Both from *Protestantism: A Symposium* edited by William K. Anderson. Copyright 1944 by Commission on Courses of Study, The Methodist Church.

The Right Reverend Angus Dun for "The Evangelical Heritage" and excerpts from "Some Evangelical Convictions" from *The Protestant Episcopal Standard*. Permission granted by Bishop Dun.

The Encyclopaedia Britannica Company for quotation from a letter from New England, "Words Carved on a Harvard Gate" from *Encyclopaedia Britannica*, 11th Edn.

Harcourt, Brace & World, Inc. for "Pigeon Church" and "The Bible and Abraham Lincoln" from *Abraham Lincoln: The Prairie Years*, Vol. I, by Carl Sandburg. Copyright 1926 by Harcourt, Brace & Co., Inc. Permission granted by Harcourt, Brace & World, Inc.

Harper & Row, Publishers, and Walter Russell Bowie for "Angels from Britain," "The Monasteries," and "John Wesley," from *Men of Fire* by Walter Russell Bowie. Copyright 1961 by Walter Russell Bowie. For "The Beginnings of Christianity" from *A History of Christianity* by Kenneth Scott Latourette. Copyright 1953 by Harper & Brothers.

John Knox Press for "Education in America" by Benjamin Rice Lacy, Jr., a portion of "A Dynamic Tradition," Chapter VIII, and "The Protestant Spirit" by Donald G. Miller, a portion of "In the Word Incarnate," Chapter III of *Our Protestant Heritage* by Members of the Faculty of Union Theological Seminary in Virginia. Copyright 1948 by John Knox Press.

The Right Reverend Arthur Lichtenberger for "A Message to the Church." Permission granted by Bishop Lichtenberger.

Marcus L. Loane for "An English Bible" from *Masters of the English Reformation* by Marcus L. Loane. Published by The Church Book Room Press 1954. Permission granted by the author.

The Macmillan Company for "Sunday Dress" from *Twenty Years at Hull House* by Jane Addams. Copyright 1910 by The Macmillan Company. Copyright 1938 by James W. Linn. Reprinted with the permission of the publisher. For "General William Booth Enters Into Heaven" by Vachel Lindsay. Reprinted with the permission of The Macmillan Company from *General William Booth Enters Into Heaven and Other Poems* by Vachel Lindsay. Copyright 1913 by The Macmillan Company.

T. & T. Clark for "A Definition" from *Encyclopaedia of Religion and Ethics*. T. & T. Clark, publishers for world rights excluding the United States.

The Bodley Head Ltd. for "The Second Crucifixion" by Richard Le Gallienne from *Robert Louis Stevenson: An Elegy and Other Poems*, published by John Lane, The Bodley Head Ltd.

H. V. Morton and Dodd, Mead & Company for "The Holy Thorn" from *In Search of England* by H. V. Morton. Copyright 1935 by Dodd, Mead & Company. Permission granted by H. V. Morton.

The National Council of Churches for the Scripture quotations in this publication from the *Revised Standard Version of the Bible*. Copyright 1946, 1952 by the Division of Christian Education, National Council of Churches, and used by permission.

Mrs. Celeste Phelps Osgood for "Puritans" from *Autobiography* by William Lyon Phelps. Published by Oxford University Press, 1939. Copyright 1939 by William Lyon Phelps. Permission granted by Mrs. Osgood as niece and heir to William Lyon Phelps.

Oxford University Press, Inc. for "What Is Protestantism" from *The Spirit of Protestantism* by Robert McAfee Brown. Copyright 1961 by Oxford University Press, Inc. For quotation from the words of Martin Luther from *The Christian Tradition and the Unity We Seek* by Albert C. Outler. Copyright 1957 by Oxford University Press.

Henry Mahler and *Presbyterian Life* for "The Rude Trumpet" by Henry Mahler. Reprinted from *Presbyterian Life* with the permission of the publisher and the author.

Charles Scribner's Sons for "George Whitefield in Connecticut" by A Middletown Farmer and "Keeping the Sabbath" by Henry Ward Beecher, both reprinted with the permission of Charles Scribner's Sons from *The Church of Our Fathers* by Roland H. Bainton. Copyright 1941

Charles Scribner's Sons, copyright 1950 R. H. Bainton. For "The Religion of Robert E. Lee" reprinted with the permission of Charles Scribner's Sons from *R. E. Lee*, Vol. IV, pp. 503–4, by Douglas Southall Freeman. Copyright 1935 Charles Scribner's Sons; renewal copyright © 1963 Inez Goddin Freeman. For "A Definition" from *Encyclopaedia of Religion and Ethics*. Copyright 1919 by Charles Scribner's Sons. For quotation "From the Words of Martin Luther" from *A History of the Reformation*, Vol. I by Thomas M. Lindsay. Copyright 1906 by Charles Scribner's Sons. For quotation from the words of John Huss from *The Church* by John Huss, tr. by David S. Schaff. Published 1915 by Charles Scribner's Sons. For "The Execution of John Huss of Bohemia" by David S. Schaff from Vol. V, Part II, *The Middle Ages of the History of the Christian Church*, edited by Philip Schaff. Copyright 1910 by Charles Scribner's Sons.

The Society of Authors for extracts from *Saint Joan* by [George] Bernard Shaw. Copyright 1924 by Brentano's. Permission granted by The Public Trustee and The Society of Authors.

Time, the Weekly Newsmagazine for "The New Evangelist" Reprinted by courtesy of *Time*. Copyright 1954, Time Inc.

The University of Chicago Press for "The Contribution of Protestantism" from *The Protestant Era* by Paul Tillich. Copyright 1948 by The University of Chicago.

Random House, Inc. for quotations from the writings of John Wyclif from *Great Voices of the Reformation* by Harry Emerson Fosdick. Copyright 1952 by Random House, Inc.

Cambridge University Press for "Thomas Carlyle" from *The Protestant Tradition* by J. S. Whale, published 1955 by Cambridge University Press.

Contents

Introduction

This is a book that begins a very long time ago and continues on to today. It actually begins with the beginnings of man himself and is the story of his search for answers to questions that repeat themselves over and over in the hearts of each generation.

Why am I here?
Where did I come from?
Where am I going?
What is right?
What is wrong?

For most of us, the answers to these questions have been found in what we call religion. For the Western world in which we live, religion rests upon a common foundation of faith which undergirds the various denominations.

That foundation is the body of history and hope known as the Old Testament. The teachings held out to the Jews the promise of a Messiah, a deliverer who would come to fulfill God's saving purpose for his people. Christians believe that this promise was kept with the birth of Jesus Christ, whose life and the influence which flowed from it added the New Testament to the Old Testament.

Christ, through His disciples, also founded a Church in which all Christians claim membership. For hundreds of years, that Church and its fellowship in which all Christians worshiped were the same. Then, because men disagreed in their thinking about some of the things that Jesus and His disciples had taught and because men developed different ideas about how God should be worshiped, many Christians went separate and different ways.

So there came the divisions which are represented now by such church names as Episcopal, Lutheran, Presbyterian, Baptist, Methodist, Reformed, and many others. These divisions stem from the great spiritual movement of the sixteenth century known as the Reformation, which broke the organizational unity that had its center in the Church at Rome. Differing from Roman Catholicism, the churches which directly felt the spirit of the Reformation are known as *Protestant*. It is this experience and the essential faith which these Christians hold in common that are the subject of this book.

We should remember, at this point, that Protestants, particularly Episcopalians and Lutherans, share many of their Christian beliefs not only with Roman Catholics but also with the members of the Orthodox churches. These churches, originating in Eastern Europe and in the Near East, were separate from the Church of Rome long before anyone even coined the term "Protestant." However, they are closer to the Roman Catholic Church than most Protestant churches and do not directly express the Protestant tradition.

That tradition is a long and noble one. No book of this size can offer you more than a sampling of it. But if it tempts you, if you are a Protestant, to learn more about your own faith, or, if you are Catholic, Jewish, or Orthodox, to learn more about the faith of your fellow citizens, it will have served its purpose.

2

It is the best gift God has given to man.

Abraham Lincoln (1809–65)

The Jewish Promise

Throughout history the Jews have been known as "the people of the Book." That book is the Bible which, for them, consists first of what is referred to as the Law, or the Torah. This is also known as the Pentateuch, the first five books of the Old Testament, which tell us the stories of the creation of man: Adam and Eve and their expulsion from the Garden of Eden; Cain and Abel and their quarrel; Noah and the flood; the Tower of Babel; the patriarchs, Abraham, Isaac, and Jacob; Joseph in Egypt; and the story of Moses and Aaron and how they led Joseph's descendants from Egypt to the Promised Land; the giving of the Ten Commandments and other directions for life and worship which the Jewish people accepted as the word of God.

The rest of the Old Testament carries on the history of the Jews, and in it we find the familiar stories of Joshua and the fall of Jericho; Samson and Delilah; of Saul's plot against David and David's friendship with Jonathan; the slaying of Goliath; the building of the Temple by Solomon; the defeat of Haman by Esther; the troubles of Job; the fall of Jerusalem; the captivity in Babylon; Daniel in the lion's den; and many others.

But the Old Testament is not only a narrative of Jewish his-

3

tory. It is poetry and proverbs and wisdom and prophecy. What follows is something of all of these, and if you read carefully you will find the promise of the coming of Christ.

FROM THE PSALMS

The LORD is a stronghold for the oppressed,
    a stronghold in times of trouble.
And those who know thy name put their trust in thee,
    for thou, O LORD, hast not forsaken those who seek thee.

The LORD is my light and my salvation;
    whom shall I fear?
The LORD is the stronghold of my life;
    of whom shall I be afraid?

O taste and see that the LORD is good!
    Happy is the man who takes refuge in him!

As a hart longs
    for flowing streams,
so longs my soul
    for thee, O God.
My soul thirsts for God,
    for the living God.
When shall I come and behold
    the face of God?

God is our refuge and strength,
    a very present help in trouble.
Therefore we will not fear though the earth should change,
    though the mountains shake in the heart of the sea;
though its waters roar and foam,
    though the mountains tremble with its tumult.   *Selah*

There is a river whose streams make glad the city of God,
 the holy habitation of the Most High.

Create in me a clean heart, O God,
 and put a new and right spirit within me.
Cast me not away from the presence,
 and take not the holy Spirit from me.
Restore to me the joy of thy salvation,
 and uphold me with a willing spirit.

For thou hast no delight in sacrifice;
 were I to give a burnt offering, thou wouldst not be pleased.

The sacrifice acceptable to God is a broken spirit;
 a broken and contrite heart, O God, thou wilt not despise.

For God alone my soul waits in silence;
 from him comes my salvation.
He only is my rock and my salvation,
 my fortress; I shall not be greatly moved.

The Lord is merciful and gracious,
 slow to anger and abounding in steadfast love.
He will not always chide,
 nor will he keep his anger for ever.
He does not deal with us according to our sins,
 nor requite us according to our iniquities.
For as the heavens are high above the earth,
 so great is his steadfast love toward those who fear him;
as far as the east is from the west,
 so far does he remove our transgressions from us.
As a father pities his children,
 so the Lord pities those who fear him.
For he knows our frame;
 he remembers that we are dust.

FROM THE BOOK OF ISAIAH

Wash yourselves; make yourselves clean;
  remove the evil of your doings
  from before my eyes;
cease to do evil,
  learn to do good;
seek justice,
  correct oppression;
defend the fatherless,
  plead for the widow.

Come now, let us reason together,
  says the LORD:
though your sins are like scarlet,
  they shall be as white as snow;
though they are red like crimson,
  they shall become like wool.

For unto us a child is born, unto us a son is given: and the government shall be upon his shoulder: and his name shall be called Wonderful, Counsellor, The mighty God, The everlasting Father, The Prince of Peace.

Of the increase of *his* government and peace *there shall be* no end, upon the throne of David, and upon his kingdom, to order it, and to establish it with judgment and with justice from henceforth even for ever. The zeal of the LORD of hosts will perform this.

And there shall come forth a rod out of the stem of Jesse, and a Branch shall grow out of his roots:

And the spirit of the LORD shall rest upon him, the spirit of wisdom and understanding, the spirit of counsel and might, the spirit of knowledge and of the fear of the LORD;

And shall make him of quick understanding in the fear of the LORD: and he shall not judge after the sight of his eyes, neither reprove after the hearing of his ears:

But with righteousness shall he judge the poor, and reprove with equity for the meek of the earth: and he shall smite the earth with the rod of his mouth, and with the breath of his lips shall he slay the wicked.

And righteousness shall be the girdle of his loins, and faithfulness the girdle of his reins.

Strengthen the weak hands,
   and make firm the feeble knees.
Say to those who are of a fearful heart,
   "Be strong, fear not!
Behold, your God
   will come with vengeance,
and with the recompense of God.
   He will come and save you."

Then the eyes of the blind shall be opened,
   and the ears of the deaf unstopped;
then shall the lame man leap like a hart,
   and the tongue of the dumb sing for joy.
For waters shall break forth in the wilderness,
   and streams in the desert;
the burning sand shall become a pool,
   and the thirsty ground springs of water;
the haunt of jackals shall become a swamp,
   the grass shall become reeds and rushes.

Comfort, comfort my people,
   says your God.
Speak tenderly to Jerusalem,
   and cry to her
that her warfare is ended,
   that her iniquity is pardoned,
that she has received from the LORD's hand
   double for all her sins.

A voice cries:
"In the wilderness prepare the way of the LORD,
   make straight in the desert a highway for our God.
Every valley shall be lifted up,
   and every mountain and hill be made low;
the uneven ground shall become level,
   and the rough places a plain.
And the glory of the LORD shall be revealed,
   and all flesh shall see it together,
   for the mouth of the LORD has spoken."

A voice says, "Cry!"
   And I said, "What shall I cry?"
All flesh is grass,
   and all its beauty is like the flower of the field.
The grass withers, the flower fades,
   when the breath of the LORD blows upon it;
surely the people is grass.
The grass withers, the flower fades;
   but the word of our God will stand for ever.
Get you up to a high mountain,
   O Zion, herald of good tidings;
lift up your voice with strength,
   O Jerusalem, herald of good tidings,

9

lift it up, fear not;
say to the cities of Judah,
  "Behold your God!"
Behold, the Lord God comes with might,
  and his arm rules for him;
behold, his reward is with him,
  and his recompense before him.
He will feed his flock like a shepherd,
  he will gather the lambs in his arms,
he will carry them in his bosom,
  and gently lead those that are with young.

Have you not known? Have you not heard?
The Lord is the everlasting God,
  the Creator of the ends of the earth.
He does not faint or grow weary,
  his understanding is unsearchable.
He gives power to the faint,
  and to him who has no might he increases strength.
Even youths shall faint and be weary,
  and young men shall fall exhausted;
but they who wait for the Lord shall renew their strength,
  they shall mount up with wings like eagles,
they shall run and not be weary,
  they shall walk and not faint.

How beautiful upon the mountains
  are the feet of him who brings good tidings,
who publishes peace, who brings good tidings of good,
  who publishes salvation,
  who says to Zion, "Your God reigns."
Hark, your watchmen lift up their voice,
  together they sing for joy;
for eye to eye they see
  the return of the Lord to Zion.

Break forth together into singing,
   you waste places of Jerusalem;
for the Lord has comforted his people,
   he has redeemed Jerusalem.
The Lord has bared his holy arm
   before the eyes of all the nations;
and all the ends of the earth shall see
   the salvation of our God.

   Who hath believed our report? and to whom is the arm of the Lord revealed?

   For he shall grow up before him as a tender plant, and as a root out of a dry ground: he hath no form nor comeliness, and when we shall see him, *there is* no beauty that we should desire him.

   He is despised and rejected of men; a man of sorrows, and acquainted with grief: and we hid as it were *our* faces from him; he was despised, and we esteemed him not.

   Surely he hath borne our griefs, and carried our sorrows: yet we did esteem him stricken, smitten of God, and afflicted.

   But he *was* wounded for our transgressions, *he was* bruised for our iniquities: the chastisement of our peace *was* upon him; and with his stripes we are healed.

   All we like sheep have gone astray; we have turned every one to his own way; and the Lord hath laid on him the iniquity of us all.

   He was oppressed, and he was afflicted, yet he opened not his mouth: he is brought as a lamb to the slaughter, and as a sheep before his shearers is dumb, so he openeth not his mouth.

   He was taken from prison and from judgment: and who shall declare his generation? for he was cut off out of the land of the living: for the transgression of my people was he stricken.

   And he made his grave with the wicked, and with the rich in his death; because he had done no violence, neither *was any* deceit in his mouth.

Yet it pleased the LORD to bruise him; he hath put *him* to grief: when thou shalt make his soul an offering for sin, he shall see *his* seed, he shall prolong *his* days, and the pleasure of the LORD shall prosper in his hand.

He shall see of the travail of his soul, *and* shall be satisfied: by his knowledge shall my righteous servant justify many; for he shall bear their iniquities.

"Ho, every one who thirsts,
 come to the waters;
and he who has no money,
 come, buy and eat!
Come, buy wine and milk
 without money and without price.
Why do you spend your money for that which is not bread,
 and your labor for that which does not satisfy?
Hearken diligently to me, and eat what is good,
 and delight yourselves in fatness.
Incline your ear, and come to me;
 hear, that your soul may live;
and I will make with you an everlasting covenant,
 my steadfast, sure love for David."

Behold, you shall call nations that you know not,
 and nations that knew you not shall run to you,
because of the LORD your God, and of the Holy One of Israel,
 for he has glorified you.

"Seek the LORD while he may be found,
 call upon him while he is near;
let the wicked forsake his way,
 and the unrighteous man his thoughts;
let him return to the LORD, that he may have mercy on him,
 and to our God, for he will abundantly pardon."
For thus says the high and lofty One
 who inhabits eternity, whose name is Holy:

"I dwell in the high and holy place,
   and also with him who is of a contrite and humble spirit,
to revive the spirit of the humble,
   and to revive the heart of the contrite."

The spirit of the Lord God is upon me
   because the Lord has anointed me
to bring good tidings to the afflicted;
   he has sent me to bind up the brokenhearted,
to proclaim liberty to the captives,
   and the opening of the prison to those who are bound;
to proclaim the year of the Lord's favor,
   and the day of vengeance of our God;
   to comfort all who mourn;
to grant to those who mourn in Zion—
   to give them a garland instead of ashes,
the oil of gladness instead of mourning,
   the mantle of praise instead of a faint spirit;
that they may be called oaks of righteousness,
   the planting of the Lord, that he may be glorified.

FROM THE BOOK OF JEREMIAH

For I will satisfy the weary soul, and every languishing soul I will replenish.

But this is the covenant which I will make with the house of Israel after those days, says the LORD: "I will put my law within them, and I will write it upon their hearts; and I will be their God, and they shall be my people. And no longer shall each man teach his neighbor and each his brother, saying, 'Know the LORD,' for they shall all know me, from the least of them to the greatest, says the LORD; for I will forgive their iniquity, and I will remember their sin no more."

FROM THE BOOK OF MICAH

But thou, Bethlehem Ephratah, *though* thou be little among the thousands of Judah, *yet* out of thee shall he come forth unto me *that is* to be ruler in Israel; whose goings forth *have been* from old, from everlasting.

14

FROM THE BOOK OF HABAKKUK

And the Lord answered me:
"Write the vision;
   make it plain upon tablets,
   so he may run who reads it.
For still the vision awaits its time;
   it hastens to the end—it will not lie.
If it seem slow, wait for it;
   it will surely come, it will not delay.
Behold, he whose soul is not upright in him shall fail,
   but the righteous shall live by his faith."

One English book and one only,
where . . . perfect plainness of speech
is allied with perfect nobleness; and
that book is the Bible.
                    Matthew Arnold (1822–88)

The Coming of Christ

For those of us whose native tongue is English, the Bible is best known to us in the words of what is called the King James Version. This translation, which was first published in 1611, was based upon the best Hebrew and Greek manuscripts then available, and upon the Latin translation which was made by St. Jerome in the fourth century.

Yet the Old Testament was written in Hebrew and a later language called Aramaic; the Jews made translations into Greek. And the New Testament was written in Greek; but St. Jerome's translation into Latin became the standard version for the early Roman Church.

The King James Version is a Protestant version; but there are a number of other Protestant versions in English as well as many Catholic and Jewish versions. As new knowledge about Biblical times becomes available (the discovery of the Dead Sea scrolls is one such example), scholars are able to produce new translations which may be closer to their originals than those we know best. There is little disagreement among Bible scholars of the major faiths and some day there may be a version of the Bible upon which all faiths will agree.

Almost all of the Old Testament passages in this book were taken from the Revised Standard Version, a recent translation by American scholars used in many American churches. But the story of Jesus, his life, his death and what that life and death meant to the people of his time (as well as those who came after) is here told in the long-familiar words of the King James Version. From that version also are the passages from the Book of Acts, from the Epistle to the Galatians, and from the First Epistle to the Corinthians.

In reading the King James Version it will be noted that a number of words are printed in italics. This was not for the purpose of giving special emphasis to those words. On the contrary, it was a device used by the translators to indicate that words not in the original manuscripts had been supplied, in order to make complete English sentences.

FROM THE GOSPELS

(Rearranged in chronological order)

Now the birth of Jesus Christ was on this wise: When as his mother Mary was espoused to Joseph, before they came together, she was found with child of the Holy Ghost.

Then Joseph her husband, being a just *man*, and not willing to make her a publick example, was minded to put her away privily.

But while he thought on these things, behold, the angel of the Lord appeared unto him in a dream, saying, Joseph, thou son of David, fear not to take unto thee Mary thy wife: for that which is conceived in her is of the Holy Ghost.

And she shall bring forth a son, and thou shalt call his name JESUS: for he shall save his people from their sins.

And it came to pass in those days, that there went out a decree from Caesar Augustus, that all the world should be taxed.

(*And* this taxing was first made when Cyrenius was governor of Syria.)

And all went to be taxed, every one to his own city.

And Joseph also went up from Galilee, out of the city of Nazareth, into Judaea, unto the city of David, which is called Bethlehem; (because he was of the house and lineage of David:)

To be taxed with Mary his espoused wife, being great with child.

And so it was, that, while they were there, the days were accomplished that she should be delivered.

And she brought forth her firstborn son, and wrapped him in swaddling clothes, and laid him in a manger; because there was no room for them in the inn.

19

And there were in the same country shepherds abiding in the field, keeping watch over their flock by night.

And, lo, the angel of the Lord came upon them, and the glory of the Lord shone round about them: and they were sore afraid.

And the angel said unto them, Fear not: for, behold, I bring you good tidings of great joy, which shall be to all people.

For unto you is born this day in the city of David a Saviour, which is Christ the Lord.

And this *shall be* a sign unto you; Ye shall find the babe wrapped in swaddling clothes, lying in a manger.

And suddenly there was with the angel a multitude of the heavenly host praising God, and saying,

Glory to God in the highest, and on earth peace, good will toward men.

And it came to pass, as the angels were gone away from them into heaven, the shepherds said one to another, Let us now go even unto Bethlehem, and see this thing which is come to pass, which the Lord hath made known unto us.

And they came with haste, and found Mary, and Joseph, and the babe lying in a manger.

And when they had seen *it*, they made known abroad the saying which was told them concerning this child.

And all they that heard *it* wondered at those things which were told them by the shepherds.

But Mary kept all these things, and pondered them in her heart.

And the shepherds returned, glorifying and praising God for all the things that they had heard and seen, as it was told unto them.

Now when Jesus was born in Bethlehem of Judaea in the days of Herod the king, behold, there came wise men from the east to Jerusalem,

Saying, Where is he that is born King of the Jews? for we have seen his star in the east, and are come to worship him.

When Herod the king had heard *these things*, he was troubled, and all Jerusalem with him.

And when he had gathered all the chief priests and scribes of the people together, he demanded of them where Christ should be born.

And they said unto him, In Bethlehem of Judaea: for thus it is written by the prophet,

And thou Bethlehem, *in* the land of Judah, art not the least among the princes of Judah: for out of thee shall come a Governor, that shall rule my people Israel.

Then Herod, when he had privily called the wise men, enquired of them diligently what time the star appeared.

And he sent them to Bethlehem, and said, Go and search diligently for the young child; and when ye have found *him*, bring me word again, that I may come and worship him also.

When they had heard the king, they departed; and, lo, the star, which they saw in the east, went before them, till it came and stood over where the young child was.

When they saw the star, they rejoiced with exceeding great joy.

And when they were come into the house, they saw the young child with Mary his mother, and fell down, and worshipped him: and when they had opened their treasures, they presented unto him gifts; gold, and frankincense, and myrrh.

In those days came John the Baptist, preaching in the wilderness of Judaea,

And saying, Repent ye: for the kingdom of heaven is at hand.

For this is he that was spoken of by the prophet Esaias, saying, The voice of one crying in the wilderness, Prepare ye the way of the Lord, make his paths straight.

Then cometh Jesus from Galilee to Jordan unto John, to be baptized of him.

But John forbad him, saying, I have need to be baptized of thee, and comest thou to me?

And Jesus answering said unto him, Suffer *it to be so* now: for thus it becometh us to fulfill all righteousness. Then he suffered him.

And Jesus, when he was baptized, went up straightway out of the water: and, lo, the heavens were opened unto him, and he saw the Spirit of God descending like a dove, and lighting upon him: And, lo, a voice from heaven, saying, This is my beloved Son, in whom I am well pleased.

And Jesus being full of the Holy Ghost returned from Jordan, and was led by the Spirit into the wilderness,

Being forty days tempted of the devil. And in those days he did eat nothing: and when they were ended, he afterward hungered.

And the devil said unto him, If thou be the Son of God, command this stone that it be made bread.

And Jesus answered him, saying, It is written, That man shall not live by bread alone, but by every word of God.

And the devil, taking him up into an high mountain, shewed unto him all the kingdoms of the world in a moment of time.

And the devil said unto him, All this power will I give thee, and the glory of them: for that is delivered unto me; and to whomsoever I will I give it.

If thou therefore wilt worship me, all shall be thine.

And Jesus answered and said unto him, Get thee behind me, Satan: for it is written, Thou shalt worship the Lord thy God, and him only shalt thou serve.

And he brought him to Jerusalem, and set him on a pinnacle of the temple, and said unto him, If thou be the Son of God, cast thyself down from hence:

For it is written, He shall give his angels charge over thee, to keep thee:

And in *their* hands they shall bear thee up, lest at any time thou dash thy foot against a stone.

And Jesus answering said unto him, It is said, Thou shalt not tempt the Lord thy God.

And when the devil had ended all the temptation, he departed from him for a season.

And Jesus returned in the power of the Spirit into Galilee: and there went out a fame of him through all the region round about.

And he taught in their synagogues, being glorified of all.

And he came to Nazareth, where he had been brought up: and, as his custom was, he went into the synagogue on the sabbath day, and stood up for to read.

And there was delivered unto him the book of the prophet Esaias. And when he had opened the book, he found the place where it was written,

The Spirit of the Lord *is* upon me, because he hath anointed me to preach the gospel to the poor; he hath sent me to heal the brokenhearted, to preach deliverance to the captives, and recovering of sight to the blind, to set at liberty them that are bruised,

To preach the acceptable year of the Lord.

And he closed the book, and he gave *it* again to the minister, and sat down. And the eyes of all them that were in the synagogue were fastened on him.

And he began to say unto them, This day is this scripture fulfilled in your ears.

And Jesus went out, and his disciples, into the towns of Caesarea Philippi: and by the way he asked his disciples, saying unto them, Whom do men say that I am?

And they answered, John the Baptist: but some *say*, Elias; and others, One of the prophets.

And he saith unto them, But whom say ye that I am? And Peter answereth and saith unto him, Thou art the Christ.

And he charged them that they should tell no man of him.

And he began to teach them, that the Son of man must suffer many things, and be rejected of the elders, and *of* the chief priests, and scribes, and be killed, and after three days rise again.

And seeing the multitudes, he went up into a mountain: and when he was set, his disciples came unto him:

And he opened his mouth, and taught them, saying,

Blessed *are* the poor in spirit: for theirs is the kingdom of heaven.

Blessed *are* they that mourn: for they shall be comforted.

Blessed *are* the meek: for they shall inherit the earth.

Blessed *are* they which do hunger and thirst after righteousness: for they shall be filled.

Blessed *are* the merciful: for they shall obtain mercy.

Blessed *are* the pure in heart: for they shall see God.

Blessed *are* the peacemakers: for they shall be called the children of God.

Blessed *are* they which are persecuted for righteousness' sake: for theirs is the kingdom of heaven.

Blessed are ye, when *men* shall revile you, and persecute *you*, and shall say all manner of evil against you falsely, for my sake.

Rejoice, and be exceeding glad: for great *is* your reward in heaven: for so persecuted they the prophets which were before you.

Ye are the salt of the earth: but if the salt have lost his savour, wherewith shall it be salted? it is thenceforth good for nothing, but to be cast out, and to be trodden under foot of men.

Ye are the light of the world. A city that is set on an hill cannot be hid.

Neither do men light a candle, and put it under a bushel, but on a candlestick; and it giveth light unto all that are in the house.

Let your light so shine before men, that they may see your good works, and glorify your Father which is in heaven.

Now the feast of unleavened bread drew nigh, which is called the Passover.

And when the hour was come, he sat down, and the twelve apostles with him.

And he said unto them, With desire I have desired to eat this Passover with you before I suffer:

For I say unto you, I will not any more eat thereof, until it be fulfilled in the kingdom of God.

And he took the cup, and gave thanks, and said, Take this, and divide *it* among yourselves:

For I say unto you, I will not drink of the fruit of the vine, until the kingdom of God shall come.

And he took bread, and gave thanks, and brake *it*, and gave unto them, saying, This is my body which is given for you: this do in remembrance of me.

Likewise also the cup after supper, saying, This cup *is* the new testament in my blood, which is shed for you.

And he came out, and went, as he was wont, to the Mount of Olives; and his disciples also followed him.

And when he was at the place, he said unto them, Pray that ye enter not into temptation.

And he was withdrawn from them about a stone's cast, and kneeled down, and prayed,

Saying, Father, if thou be willing, remove this cup from me: nevertheless not my will, but thine, be done.

And there appeared an angel unto him from heaven, strengthening him.

And while he yet spake, behold a multitude, and he that was called Judas, one of the twelve, went before them, and drew near unto Jesus to kiss him.

But Jesus said unto him, Judas, betrayest thou the Son of man with a kiss?

Then took they him, and led *him*, and brought him into the high priest's house. And Peter followed afar off.

And when they had kindled a fire in the midst of the hall, and were set down together, Peter sat down among them.

But a certain maid beheld him as he sat by the fire, and earnestly looked upon him, and said, This man was also with him.

And he denied him, saying, Woman, I know him not.

And after a little while another saw him, and said, Thou art also of them. And Peter said, Man, I am not.

And about the space of one hour after another confidently affirmed, saying, Of a truth this *fellow* also was with him: for he is a Galilaean.

And Peter said, Man, I know not what thou sayest. And immediately, while he yet spake, the cock crew.

And the Lord turned, and looked upon Peter. And Peter remembered the word of the Lord, how he had said unto him, Before the cock crow, thou shalt deny me thrice.

And Peter went out, and wept bitterly.

And the men that held Jesus mocked him, and smote *him*.

And when they had blindfolded him, they struck him on the face, and asked him, saying, Prophesy, who is it that smote thee?

And many other things blasphemously spake they against him.

And as soon as it was day, the elders of the people and the chief priests and the scribes came together, and led him into their council, saying,

Art thou the Christ? tell us. And he said unto them, If I tell you, ye will not believe:

And if I also ask *you*, ye will not answer me, nor let *me* go.

Hereafter shall the Son of man sit on the right hand of the power of God.

Then said they all, Art thou then the Son of God? And he said unto them, Ye say that I am.

And they said, What need we any further witness? for we ourselves have heard of his own mouth.

And the whole multitude of them arose, and led him unto Pilate.

And they began to accuse him, saying, "We found this *fellow* perverting the nation, and forbidding to give tribute to Caesar, saying that he himself is Christ a King."

And Pilate asked him, saying, Art thou the King of the Jews? And he answered him and said, Thou sayest *it*.

Then said Pilate to the chief priests and *to* the people, I find no fault in this man.

And they were the more fierce, saying, He stirreth up the people, teaching throughout all Jewry, beginning from Galilee to this place.

And Pilate, when he had called together the chief priests and the rulers and the people,

Said unto them, Ye have brought this man unto me, as one that perverteth the people: and, behold, I, having examined *him* before you, have found no fault in this man touching those things whereof ye accuse him:

No, nor yet Herod: for I sent you to him; and, lo, nothing worthy of death is done unto him.

I will therefore chastise him, and release *him*.

(For of necessity he must release one unto them at the feast.)

And they cried out all at once, saying, Away with this *man*, and release unto us Barabbas:

(Who for a certain sedition made in the city, and for murder, was cast into prison.)

Pilate therefore, willing to release Jesus, spake again to them.

But they cried, saying, Crucify *him*, crucify him.

And he said unto them the third time, Why, what evil hath he done? I have found no cause of death in him: I will therefore chastise him, and let *him* go.

And they were instant with loud voices, requiring that he might be crucified. And the voices of them and of the chief priests prevailed.

And Pilate gave sentence that it should be as they required.

And there were also two other malefactors, led with him to be put to death.

And when they were come to the place, which is called Calvary, there they crucified him, and the malefactors, one on the right hand, and the other on the left.

Then said Jesus, Father, forgive them; for they know not what they do. And they parted his raiment, and cast lots.

And the people stood beholding. And the rulers also with

them derided *him*, saying, He saved others; let him save himself, if he be Christ, the chosen of God.

And the soldiers also mocked him, coming to him, and offering vinegar,

And saying, If thou be the king of the Jews, save thyself.

And a superscription also was written over him in letters of Greek, and Latin, and Hebrew, THIS IS THE KING OF THE JEWS.

And one of the malefactors which were hanged railed on him, saying, If thou be Christ, save thyself and us.

But the other answering rebuked him, saying, Dost not thou fear God, seeing thou art in the same condemnation?

And we indeed justly; for we receive the due reward of our deeds: but this man hath done nothing amiss.

And he said unto Jesus, Lord, remember me when thou comest into thy kingdom.

And Jesus said unto him, Verily I say unto thee, To day shalt thou be with me in paradise.

And it was about the sixth hour, and there was a darkness over all the earth until the ninth hour.

And the sun was darkened, and the veil of the temple was rent in the midst.

And when Jesus had cried with a loud voice, he said, Father, into thy hands I commend my spirit: and having said thus, he gave up the ghost.

Now upon the first *day* of the week, very early in the morning, they came unto the sepulchre, bringing the spices which they had prepared, and certain *others* with them.

And they found the stone rolled away from the sepulchre.

And they entered in, and found not the body of the Lord Jesus.

And it came to pass, as they were much perplexed thereabout, behold, two men stood by them in shining garments:

And as they were afraid, and bowed down *their* faces to the earth, they said unto them, Why seek ye the living among the dead?

He is not here, but is risen: remember how he spake unto you when he was yet in Galilee,

Saying, The Son of man must be delivered into the hands of sinful men, and be crucified, and the third day rise again.

He is not here, but is risen: remember how he spake unto you
when he was yet in Galilee,
Saying, The Son of man must be delivered into the hands of
sinful men, and be crucified, and the third day rise again.

FROM THE ACTS OF THE APOSTLES

But Peter, standing up with the eleven, lifted up his voice, and said unto them, Ye men of Judaea, and all *ye* that dwell at Jerusalem, be this known unto you, and hearken to my words:

This Jesus hath God raised up, whereof we all are witnesses.

Therefore being by the right hand of God exalted, and having received of the Father the promise of the Holy Ghost, he hath shed forth this which ye now see and hear.

For David is not ascended into the heavens: but he saith himself, The Lord said unto my Lord, Sit thou on my right hand,

Until I make thy foes thy footstool.

Therefore let all the house of Israel know assuredly, that God hath made that same Jesus, whom ye have crucified, both Lord and Christ.

FROM THE EPISTLE OF PAUL TO THE ROMANS

For I am not ashamed of the gospel: it is the power of God for salvation to every one who has faith, to the Jew first and also to the Greek. For in it the righteousness of God is revealed through faith for faith; as it is written, "He who through faith is righteous shall live."

But now the righteousness of God has been manifested apart from law, although the law and the prophets bear witness to it, the righteousness of God through faith in Jesus Christ for all who believe. For there is no distinction;

Then what becomes of all our boasting? It is excluded. On what principle? On the principle of works? No, but on the principle of faith. For we hold that a man is justified by faith apart from works of law.

In hope he believed against hope, that he should become the father of many nations; as he had been told, "So shall your descendants be."

No distrust made him waver concerning the promise of God, but he grew strong in his faith as he gave glory to God, fully convinced that God was able to do what he had promised. That is why his faith was "reckoned to him as righteousness."

Therefore, since we are justified by faith, we have peace with God through our Lord Jesus Christ. Through him we have obtained access to this grace in which we stand, and we rejoice in our hope of sharing the glory of God.

31

FROM THE EPISTLES OF PAUL
TO THE CORINTHIANS

Moreover, brethren, I declare unto you the gospel which I preached unto you, which also ye have received, and wherein ye stand:

By which also ye are saved, if ye keep in memory what I preached unto you, unless ye have believed in vain.

For I delivered unto you first of all that which I also received, how that Christ died for our sins according to the scriptures;

And that he was buried, and that he rose again on the third day according to the scriptures:

And that he was seen of Cephas, then of the twelve:

After that, he was seen of above five hundred brethren at once; of whom the greater part remain unto this present, but some are fallen asleep.

After that, he was seen of James; then of all the apostles.

And last of all he was seen of me also, as of one born out of due time.

For I am the least of the apostles, that am not meet to be called an apostle, because I persecuted the church of God.

But by the grace of God I am what I am: and his grace which *was bestowed* upon me was not in vain; but I laboured more abundantly than they all: yet not I, but the grace of God which was with me.

Therefore whether *it were* I or they, so we preach, and so ye believed.

FROM THE EPISTLE OF PAUL
TO THE GALATIANS

Paul, an apostle, (not of men, neither by man, but by Jesus Christ, and God the Father, who raised him from the dead;) . . .

I am crucified with Christ: nevertheless I live; yet not I, but Christ liveth in me: and the life which I now live in the flesh I live by the faith of the Son of God, who loved me, and gave himself for me.

FROM THE EPISTLE TO THE HEBREWS

Now faith is the assurance of things hoped for, the conviction of things not seen.

By faith Abraham obeyed when he was called to go out to a place which he was to receive as an inheritance; and he went out, not knowing where he was to go. By faith he sojourned in the land of promise, as in a foreign land, living in tents with Isaac and Jacob, heirs with him of the same promise. For he looked forward to the city which has foundations, whose builder and maker is God.

By faith Moses, when he was grown up, refused to be called the son of Pharaoh's daughter, choosing rather to share ill-treatment with the people of God than to enjoy the fleeting pleasures

33

of sin. He considered abuse suffered for the Christ greater wealth than the treasures of Egypt, for he looked to the reward. By faith he left Egypt, not being afraid of the anger of the king; for he endured as seeing him who is invisible.

And what more shall I say? For time would fail me to tell of Gideon, Barak, Samson, Jephthah, of David and Samuel and the prophets—who through faith conquered kingdoms, enforced justice, received promises, stopped the mouths of lions, quenched raging fire, escaped the edge of the sword, won strength out of weakness, became mighty in war, put foreign armies to flight. Women received their dead by resurrection. Some were tortured, refusing to accept release, that they might rise again to a better life. Others suffered mocking and scourging, and even chains and imprisonment. They were stoned, they were sawn in two, they were killed with the sword; they went about in skins of sheep and goats, destitute, afflicted, ill-treated—of whom the world was not worthy—wandering over deserts and mountains, and in dens and caves of the earth.

And all these, though well attested by their faith, did not receive what was promised . . .

Therefore, since we are surrounded by so great a cloud of witnesses, let us also lay aside every weight, and sin which clings so closely, and let us run with perseverance the race that is set before us, looking to Jesus the pioneer and perfecter of our faith, who for the joy that was set before him endured the cross, despising the shame, and is seated at the right hand of the throne of God.

34

simple people whose faith was innocent yet great. And it was
a time for scholars who, laboring in their monasteries, passed
on to us much of the learning which we have today.

*Out of that vast tomb Christianity
issued to supersede the Caesars.*
Lew Wallace (1827–1905)

The Growth of Faith

The death of Jesus on the Cross was the first of many deaths
for a faith in which men believed so strongly. Peter was martyred
in Rome and Paul followed him to death under Nero, tradition
tells us. In the short years between, Christian congregations came
into being not only among the Jews of Palestine but also among
gentiles in Egypt, Cyprus, Asia Minor, Macedonia, Greece, and
Italy. By the time that John, who lived longest of all the Apostles,
died, the new faith had spread to nearly all parts of the Greek and
Roman worlds.

Christians suffered cruel persecutions beyond belief, but their
faith survived and continued to spread. It spread into France,
into Germany, into England, into Ireland. The Western world
was now a Christian world. The Bishop of Rome, who had begun
to claim headship in the Church and to be called the Pope, was
more than just an important religious figure; he was an important
political figure.

Popes and priests became involved in politics. Kings and emperors were now involved in religion. The Church became a
powerful institution. But it was also a time for saints and for

simple people whose faith was innocent yet great. And it was a time for scholars who, laboring in their monasteries, passed on to us much of the learning which we have today.

THE BEGINNINGS OF CHRISTIANITY

KENNETH SCOTT LATOURETTE

One of the most amazing and significant facts of history is that within five centuries of its birth, Christianity won the professed allegiance of the overwhelming majority of the population of the Roman Empire and even the support of the Roman state. Beginning as a seemingly obscure sect of Judaism, one of scores, even hundreds of religions and religious groups which were competing within that realm, revering as its central figure one who had been put to death by the machinery of Rome, and in spite of having been long proscribed by that government and eventually having the full weight of the state thrown against it, Christianity proved so far the victor that the Empire sought alliance with it and to be a Roman citizen became almost identical with being a Christian.

Outstanding in carrying the faith into the non-Jewish, and especially the Hellenistic, world was a Jew whose conversion is closely associated with the death of Stephen. This was Saul, or, to use the name by which he is best remembered, Paul. We know more about Paul than we do of any other Christian of the first century.

Christianity quickly moved out of the Jewish community and became prevailingly non-Jewish. As early as the time Paul wrote his letter to it, a generation or less after the resurrection, the church in Rome was predominantly Gentile. This in itself was highly significant: Christianity had ceased to be a Jewish sect and, while having roots in Judaism, was clearly new and different from that faith.

It is one of the commonplaces of history that in its first three centuries Christianity met persistent and often severe persecution, persecution which rose to a crescendo early in the fourth century, but that it spread in spite of opposition and was even strengthened by it.

By the close of its first five centuries Christianity had become the professed faith of the overwhelming majority of the population of the Roman Empire.

Why was it that Christianity had this amazing expansion? How shall we account for the fact that, beginning as what to the casual observer must have appeared a small and obscure sect of Judaism, before its first five centuries were out it had become the faith of the Roman state and of the vast majority of the population of that realm and had spread eastward as far as Central Asia and probably India and Ceylon and westward into far away Ireland? Why of all the many faiths which were competing for the allegiance of the Roman Empire, many of them with a much more promising outlook, did it emerge victor? Why, of all the Jewish sects, did it alone move outside the pale of Judaism and attract the millions of many races and cultures which composed the Mediterranean world?

Better than its rivals, Christianity gave to the Graeco-Roman world what so many were craving from a religion. To those wishing immortality it pointed to the historic Jesus, risen from the dead, and to the promise that those who believed in him would share with him in glorified, eternal life. To those demanding high morality it offered standards beyond the full attainment of men and the power to grow towards them. To those craving fellowship it presented a community of worship and of mutual aid, with care for the poor, the infirm, and the aged. To those who, distrustful of reason, longed for a faith sanctioned by immemorial antiquity, it pointed out the long record preserved in what it termed the Old Testament, going back to Moses and beyond him and pointing forward to Christ. To those demanding intellectual

38

satisfaction it could present literature prepared by some of the ablest minds of the day.

Whence came these qualities which won for Christianity its astounding victory? Careful and honest investigation can give but one answer, Jesus. It was faith in Jesus and his resurrection which gave birth to the Christian fellowship and which continued to be its inspiration and its common tie. It was the love displayed in Christ which was, ideally and to a marked extent in practice, the bond which held Christians together. The early disciples unite in declaring that it was from the command of Jesus that the Gospel was proclaimed to all, regardless of sex, race, or cultural background. The new life in Christ might express itself in many forms, but its authenticity was to be proved by high, uncompromising moral qualities as set forth by Jesus.

THE HOLY THORN

H. V. MORTON

It is so quiet here. The shadows of the yews lie in long pencils over the smooth grass, but—stay—it is not so smooth! There are grassy dips and terraces where once ran altar steps. From tree to tree is a chain of bird song. Rising sheer from the grass, appalling in its appealing starkness, is the great arch of the central tower of Glastonbury Abbey, the two piers rising into the air, but not to meet; there is blue sky between, and on the high, cleft towers grass is growing. This with a few tumbled walls and the beautiful St. Mary's Chapel represent all that remains of the once mighty Abbey, the elder brother of Westminster and the birthplace of Christianity in England.

. . . this quiet field is the only spot in England linked by legend with a man who knew Jesus Christ. For centuries men believed that in A.D. 61 St. Philip sent Joseph of Arimathaea, whose hands had laid Christ in the tomb, to preach the Gospel in England. He is said, according to the later legend, to have come with a band of missionaries bearing the Chalice of the Last Supper, which he had begged of Pilate. This Chalice had held the Sacred Blood from the Cross. Here in this English meadow Joseph of Arimathaea is said to have built England's first church of plaited oziers.

When the missionaries crossed Weary-all Hill ("weary-all" with the journey), Joseph, so the famous old story goes, planted his staff in the earth. It took root and grew into the famous Glastonbury Thorn.

That belief founded the international fame of Glastonbury; for centuries it was an English Jerusalem, one of the holiest places on earth. Men came from the ends of the world to pluck a sprig of the Holy Thorn in order that it might be buried with them. Saints were gathered to Glastonbury to lie in its earth. The bones of Arthur and Guinevere are said to have been buried beneath the high altar. Behind the abbey at the foot of the Tor still springs the mineral spring which was one of the wonders of the world. Its waters, heavily impregnated with iron, color the earth, and everything they touch, a rusty red; and this is the place to which the medieval pilgrim knelt trembling and crying—as I have seen pilgrims tremble and cry in Jerusalem—believing that here was buried the Holy Grail.

"See that bush? That's the Holy Thorn! The original one was hacked down by a Puritan who got a splinter in his eye from it and died. There are several offshoots round Glastonbury, and you'd be surprised at the number of slips we send away. One is going to a big church they are building in New York. We sent one to America not long ago for the tomb of President Wilson."

The grass has come back to the altar of Glastonbury, but the Holy Thorn still lives!

ANGELS FROM BRITAIN

WALTER RUSSELL BOWIE

One day in Rome, the Benedictine monk Gregory saw a sale of slaves who had been brought from Britain, where in the continual collision between earlier and later invaders—Angles, Saxons, Jutes and Danes—captives taken in the tribal battles were marketed as men had been marketed ever since the days of imperial Rome. Struck by the appearance of these particular men and boys, Gregory asked who they were, and he was told that they were Angles. "They are well named," he said, "for they must become brethren of the angels in heaven." So when he had become bishop he commissioned Augustine—not, of course, the great Augustine of Hippo, but a man of the same name—to set out with a group of companions to preach the gospel in what now is England.

Making their slow way on foot from Italy through Gaul and finally to the coast, Augustine and his companions crossed the Channel and landed in the southeastern part of England which was then the kingdom of Kent. Ethelbert, the king, was a pagan; but his queen, who had come from Gaul, was already a Christian. After a time Ethelbert himself was converted and baptized; and Augustine found a place to live and work, at the little church of St. Martin, near Canterbury, where Bertha the queen was accustomed to worship. There had been Christians in Kent in earlier centuries, but most of Christianity in the east of England had been overrun and nearly obliterated by the pagan invaders from across the sea. Now the Christian church would be reestablished, and Canterbury would become the shrine and center of continuous Christian witness, down to and through the Reformation, by which the whole history of England would be molded, and the heritage of which would be carried from England to the New World.

THE MONASTERIES

WALTER RUSSELL BOWIE

In the second century, Irenaeus, Bishop of Lyons in Gaul, looking out upon the facts of the general life, said of the order and stability which had been created by the rule of Rome: "The world is at peace, and we walk on the highways without fear, and sail where we will."

Two hundred years later the kind of world that Irenaeus knew was disappearing. The barbarian tribes from north of the Rhine and the Danube had broken the defenses of the empire and disrupted the civilization which for so long had been safeguarded by what men thought of as "the eternal city." Rome itself had fallen; and with its central power broken, life throughout the empire lost its cohesion and dissolved like sand in a flooding river. The invading tribes had no concern for the culture which the patient, creative centuries had evolved. Conquest and plunder were all that they cared about at first. The great Roman roads disintegrated, the flow of commerce and communication was cut off, the aqueducts were broken, and paralysis fell upon the life of what had been the cities. In the open country, weeds grew in the fields no longer cultivated, and around the half-abandoned villages could be heard the howling of wolves when the sun went down. People huddling together to keep alive had little chance to preserve what they might have cherished: schools, works of art, the rich resources for mind and spirit which had been familiar in the long years of the Roman peace. Over all Western Europe there fell the shadow of the Dark Ages.

One great influence beyond all others saved the future. That was the life which centered in the monasteries. Before the Roman empire fell, the monastic movement had begun. Religious commitment led many men to devote themselves—some of them fanatically—to complete withdrawal from the secular world. In the chaos which followed the barbarian invasion the numbers of those who thus withdrew increased. It was in part a despairing flight from conditions that seemed hopeless; but it carried also the indestructible spark of the will to live, from which would come a flame of hope for the years to follow. When most of civilization fell into deepening shadow, the monasteries were like little islands where even in the worst times the flickering lights of promise burned. And that light would grow stronger, and men from the monasteries would carry it out into the surrounding darkness. The activities of the mind would be revived for a world which had descended into ignorance, and the Christian evangel for men's souls carried to the invading pagan tribes.

THE HOLY ROMAN EMPIRE

WALTER RUSSELL BOWIE

In 754, nearly three hundred years after the beginning of what history has called the Dark Ages, Pope Stephen II found himself in danger. The barbarian Lombards who had settled in the north of Italy were constantly threatening Rome. Pope Stephen made a journey into France to ask for help. There he found that the army had taken its commander and made him king in place of the former king, who had been deposed and had gone into a monastery. The new king's name was Pepin, who came to be known as Pepin the Short. But whether he was short or not, he was the kind of ally the pope was looking for. He was the son of the great Charles Martel, Charles the Hammer, who had saved Europe from the Mohammedan invaders by his victory at Tours. Although Pepin was king already, the pope crowned him in the name of the Church. And he appealed to Pepin to bring his army down to Italy and teach the Lombards to behave.

So Pepin came. He marched into the Lombards' country as a conqueror. The Lombards were to let the pope alone, and they were to be punished for what they had done to him already. They should surrender five of their cities, including the ancient city of Ravenna—the city from which the last official of the emperor in Constantinople had been driven out three hundred years before. These five cities, and the country round them, Pepin gave to the pope to belong to him.

That was the beginning of something that was to make an immense difference in history for all the hundreds of years to follow. For when the pope thus had lands and cities over which he himself was the only ruler, he was no longer just a bishop of the

46

Church. His business had been to be a shepherd of the souls of men in the name of Jesus Christ. But now he was to become more and more like one of the great barons, who controlled large territories, and ordered everything that people did, and collected taxes, and grew rich. The time was soon to come when popes would seem more concerned to get more land and more power than they would be concerned to remember the words of Jesus that "whosoever of you will be the chiefest, shall be servant of all."

Not long afterward another pope was to have important dealing with another king. Pepin's son, who succeeded him, was Charles—called Charles the Great or, as it was in French, Charlemagne.

Charlemagne was brought up a Christian, and he meant to be one. He could read, which in those days not even all kings could do. The book he read most of all was Augustine's *City of God*, which told that the Church would endure when kingdoms and empires perished. Charlemagne had at his court the great scholar Alcuin, and he liked to converse with Alcuin and with other learned men. He set up schools in his kingdom, particularly in order that the clergy should get some education; and he tried to see to it that all should worship and behave themselves in the way the Church had taught.

Meanwhile at Rome, Pope Leo III was in trouble and needed help wherever he could get it. A savage gang had set upon him in the streets of the city, beaten him, and left him battered and half blind. As soon as he could, Leo went off to France to appeal to Charlemagne, as Pope Stephen had appealed to Charlemagne's father, Pepin.

Charlemagne came down to Rome to see what was the matter there and to stop the violence against the pope.

Meanwhile a new idea was working in Leo's mind. The emperor in Constantinople was far away and seemed of no use to anybody in the West. There needed to be someone big enough to have the authority that the Roman emperor used to have, and strong enough to keep the peace. Why not Charlemagne? If the

47

pope should crown him in the name of the Church, then the people would feel that it was the Church who had chosen Charlemagne and made him emperor. And Charlemagne would have to be the grateful protector of the Church.

So there came a day in the year 800 when Charlemagne went into St. Peter's Church to say his prayers. While he was kneeling there, the pope came silently up behind him. Before Charlemagne knew what was happening, the pope had placed a crown on his head. A crowd of people, instructed perhaps beforehand by the pope, shouted out their honor to "Charles, most pious and august, crowned by God, the great and peace-bringing emperor!"

Charlemagne himself was not so pleased. He would rather have arranged his own crowning than have the pope do it. He did not want it to appear that it was the pope who had given him authority when as a matter of fact it was he who had been protecting the pope. He may have foreseen that a time might come—as indeed it did—when popes would claim that emperors, like everybody else, must be servants of the Church.

But however that might be, Charlemagne had been crowned as the first head of what was called the Holy Roman Empire. That was meant to be a rulership over many countries, held together as most of the world had once been held together by the empire of Rome. But there was one difference. This was to be the *Holy* Roman Empire. It was to be side by side with the Christian Church. It was supposed to govern according to the commandments of Christ.

This Holy Roman Empire was to exist for more than a thousand years. Sometimes its emperor had much power, especially in Germany and France. Sometimes he had very little. The great question was as to who would really come nearer to being the ruler of Europe, the emperor or the pope.

*(In this story by Anatole France,
with its medieval setting, there are
phrases about the Virgin Mother which
to Protestant thought seem exagger-
ated. But the real point of the story is
in its tender conclusion that it is "the
simple-hearted" who shall see God.
This is exactly the message of the Protestant Reformation—that not only or
chiefly by ecclesiastical persons but by
all the little people in their everyday
activities God can be truly served.
—Editors)*

OUR LADY'S JUGGLER

ANATOLE FRANCE

I

In the days of King Louis there was a poor juggler in France,
a native of Compiègne, Barnaby by name, who went about from
town to town performing feats of skill and strength.

On fair days he would unfold an old worn-out carpet in the
public square, and when, by means of a jovial address, which
he had learned of a very ancient juggler, and which he never
varied in the least, he had drawn together the children and loafers,
he assumed extraordinary attitudes, and balanced a tin plate on the
tip of his nose. At first the crowd would feign indifference.

But when, supporting himself on his hands face downwards, he
threw into the air six copper balls, which glittered in the sunshine,
and caught them again with his feet; or when throwing himself

49

backwards until his heels and the nape of the neck met, giving his body the form of a perfect wheel, he would juggle in this posture with a dozen knives, a murmur of admiration would escape the spectators, and pieces of money rain down upon the carpet.

Nevertheless, like the majority of those who live by their wits, Barnaby of Compiègne had a great struggle to make a living.

Earning his bread in the sweat of his brow, he bore rather more than his share of the penalties consequent upon the misdoings of our father Adam.

Again, he was unable to work as constantly as he would have been willing to do. The warmth of the sun and the broad daylight were as necessary to enable him to display his brilliant parts as to the trees if flower and fruit should be expected of them. In winter time he was nothing more than a tree stripped of its leaves, and as it were dead. The frozen ground was hard to the juggler, and, like the grasshopper of which Marie de France tells us, the inclement season caused him to suffer both cold and hunger. But as he was simple-natured he bore his ills patiently.

He had never meditated on the origin of wealth, nor upon the inequality of human conditions. He believed firmly that, if this life should prove hard, the life to come could not fail to redress the balance, and this hope upheld him. He did not resemble those thievish and miscreant Merry Andrews who sell their souls to the devil. He never blasphemed God's name; he lived uprightly, and although he had no wife of his own, he did not covet his neighbour's, since woman is ever the enemy of the strong man, as it appears by the history of Samson recorded in the Scriptures. In truth, his was not a nature much disposed to carnal delights, and it was a greater deprivation to him to forsake the tankard than the Hebe who bore it. For, whilst not wanting in sobriety, he was fond of a drink when the weather waxed hot. He was a worthy man who feared God, and was very devoted to the Blessed Virgin.

Never did he fail on entering a church to fall upon his knees before the image of the Mother of God, and offer up this prayer to her:

"Blessed Lady, keep watch over my life until it shall please God that I die, and when I am dead, ensure to me the possession of the joys of paradise."

II

Now on a certain evening after a dreary wet day, as Barnaby pursued his road, sad and bent, carrying under his arm his balls and knives wrapped up in his old carpet, on the watch for some barn where, though he might not sup, he might sleep, he perceived on the road, going in the same direction as himself, a monk, whom he saluted courteously. And as they walked at the same rate they fell into conversation with one another.

"Fellow traveller," said the monk, "how comes it about that you are clothed all in green? Is it perhaps in order to take the part of a jester in some mystery play?"

"Not at all, good father," replied Barnaby. "Such as you see me, I am called Barnaby, and for my calling I am a juggler. There would be no pleasanter calling in the world if it would always provide one with daily bread."

"Friend Barnaby," returned the monk, "be careful what you say. There is no calling more pleasant than the monastic life. Those who lead it are occupied with the praises of God, the Blessed Virgin, and the saints; and, indeed, the religious life is one ceaseless hymn to the Lord."

Barnaby replied

"Good father, I own that I spoke like an ignorant man. Your calling cannot be in any respect compared to mine, and although there may be some merit in dancing with a penny balanced on a stick on the tip of one's nose, it is not a merit which comes within hail of your own. Gladly would I, like you, good father, sing my office day by day, and especially the office of the most Holy Virgin, to whom I have vowed a singular devotion. In order to embrace the monastic life I would willingly abandon the art by which from Soissons to Beauvais I am well known in upwards of six hundred towns and villages."

The monk was touched by the juggler's simplicity, and, as he was not lacking in discernment, he at once recognized in Barnaby

51

one of those men of whom it is said in the Scriptures: Peace on earth to men of good will. And for this reason he replied—

"Friend Barnaby, come with me, and I will have you admitted into the monastery of which I am Prior. He who guided St. Mary of Egypt in the desert set me upon your path to lead you into the way of salvation."

It was in this manner, then, that Barnaby became a monk. In the monastery into which he was received the religious vied with one another in the worship of the Blessed Virgin, and in her honour each employed all the knowledge and all the skill which God had given him.

The prior on his part wrote books dealing according to the rules of scholarship with the virtues of the Mother of God.

Brother Maurice with a deft hand copied out these treatises upon sheets of vellum.

Brother Alexander adorned the leaves with delicate miniature paintings. Here were displayed the Queen of Heaven seated upon Solomon's throne, and while four lions were on guard at her feet, around the nimbus which encircled her head hovered seven doves, which are the seven gifts of the Holy Spirit, the gifts, namely, of Fear, Piety, Knowledge, Strength, Counsel, Understanding, and Wisdom. For her companions she had six virgins with hair of gold, namely, Humility, Prudence, Seclusion, Submission, Virginity, and Obedience.

At her feet were two little naked figures, perfectly white, in an attitude of supplication. These were souls imploring her all-powerful intercession for their soul's health, and we may be sure not imploring in vain.

Upon another page facing this, Brother Alexander represented Eve, so that the Fall and the Redemption could be perceived at one and the same time—Eve the Wife abased, and Mary the Virgin exalted.

Furthermore, to the marvel of the beholder, this book contained presentments of the Well of Living Waters, the Fountain, the Lily, the Moon, the Sun, and the Garden Enclosed of which the Song of Songs tells us, the Gate of Heaven and the City of God, and all these things were symbols of the Blessed Virgin.

Brother Marbode was likewise one of the most loving children of Mary.

He spent all his days carving images in stone, so that his beard, his eyebrows, and his hair were white with dust, and his eyes continually swollen and weeping; but his strength and cheerfulness were not diminished, although he was now well gone in years, and it was clear that the Queen of Paradise still cherished her servant in his old age. Marbode represented her seated upon a throne, her brow encircled with an orb-shaped nimbus set with pearls. And he took care that the folds of her dress should cover the feet of her, concerning whom the prophet declared: My beloved is as a garden enclosed.

Sometimes, too, he depicted her in the semblance of a child full of grace, and appearing to say, "Thou art my God, even from my mother's womb."

In the priory, moreover, were poets who composed hymns in Latin, both in prose and verse, in honour of the Blessed Virgin Mary, and amongst the company was even a brother from Picardy who sang the miracles of Our Lady in rhymed verse and in the vulgar tongue.

III

Being a witness of this emulation in praise and the glorious harvest of their labours, Barnaby mourned his own ignorance and simplicity.

"Alas!" he sighed, as he took his solitary walk in the little shelterless garden of the monastery, "wretched wight that I am, to be unable, like my brothers, worthily to praise the Holy Mother of God, to whom I have vowed my whole heart's affection. Alas! alas! I am but a rough man and unskilled in the arts, and I can render you in service, blessed Lady, neither edifying sermons, nor treatises set out in order according to rule, nor ingenious paintings, nor statues truthfully sculptured, nor verses whose march is measured to the best of feet. No gift have I, alas!"

After this fashion he groaned and gave himself up to sorrow. But one evening, when the monks were spending their hour of liberty in conversation, he heard one of them tell the tale of a religious man who could repeat nothing other than the Ave Maria. This poor man was despised for his ignorance; but after his death there issued forth from his mouth five roses in honour of the five letters of the name Mary (Marie), and thus his sanctity was made manifest.

Whilst he listened to this narrative Barnaby marvelled yet once again at the loving kindness of the Virgin; but the lesson of that blessed death did not avail to console him, for his heart overflowed with zeal, and he longed to advance the glory of his Lady, who is in heaven.

How to compass this he sought but could find no way, and day by day he became the more cast down, when one morning he awakened filled full with joy, hastened to the chapel, and remained there alone for more than an hour. After dinner he returned to the chapel once more.

And, starting from that moment, he repaired daily to the chapel at such hours as it was deserted, and spent within it a good part of the time which the other monks devoted to the liberal and mechanical arts. His sadness vanished, nor did he any longer groan.

A demeanour so strange awakened the curiosity of the monks.

These began to ask one another for what purpose Brother Barnaby could be indulging so persistently in retreat.

The prior, whose duty it is to let nothing escape him in the behaviour of his children in religion, resolved to keep a watch over Barnaby during his withdrawals to the chapel. One day, then, when he was shut up there after his custom, the prior, accompanied by two of the older monks, went to discover through the chinks in the door what was going on within the chapel.

They saw Barnaby before the altar of the Blessed Virgin, head downwards, with his feet in the air, and he was juggling with six balls of copper and a dozen knives. In honour of the Holy Mother of God he was performing those feats, which aforetime had won him most renown. Not recognizing that the simple fellow was thus placing at the service of the Blessed Virgin his knowledge and skill, the two old monks exclaimed against the sacrilege.

54

The prior was aware how stainless was Barnaby's soul, but he concluded that he had been seized with madness. They were all three preparing to lead him swiftly from the chapel, when they saw the Blessed Virgin descend the steps of the altar and advance to wipe away with a fold of her azure robe the sweat which was dropping from her juggler's forehead.

Then the prior, falling upon his face upon the pavement, uttered these words—

"Blessed are the simple-hearted, for they shall see God."

"Amen!" responded the old brethren, and kissed the ground.

FROM SAINT JOAN

GEORGE BERNARD SHAW

CAUCHON. Come! We are wasting time on trifles. Joan: I am going to put a most solemn question to you. Take care how you answer; for your life and salvation are at stake on it. Will you for all you have said and done, be it good or bad, accept the judgment of God's Church on earth? More especially as to the acts and words that are imputed to you in this trial by the Promoter here, will you submit your case to the inspired interpretation of the Church Militant?

JOAN. I am a faithful child of the Church. I will obey the Church—

CAUCHON [*hopefully leaning forward*]. You will?

JOAN. —Provided it does not command anything impossible.

Cauchon sinks back in his chair with a heavy sigh. The Inquisitor purses his lips and frowns. Ladvenu shakes his head pitifully.

D'ESTIVET. She imputes to the Church the error and folly of commanding the impossible.

JOAN. If you command me to declare that all that I have done and said, and all the visions and revelations I have had, were not from God, then that is impossible: I will not declare it for anything in the world. What God made me do I will never go back on; and what He has commanded or shall command I will not fail to do in spite of any man alive. That is what I mean by impossible. And in case the Church should bid me do anything contrary to the command I have from God, I will not consent to it, no matter what it may be.

56

LADVENU [*pleading with her urgently*]. You do not know what you are saying, child. Do you want to kill yourself? Listen. Do you not believe that you are subject to the Church of God on earth?

JOAN. Yes. When have I ever denied it?

LADVENU. Good. That means, does it not, that you are subject to our Lord the Pope, to the cardinals, the archbishops, and the bishops for whom his lordship stands here today?

JOAN. God must be served first.

D'ESTIVET. Then your voices command you not to submit yourself to the Church Militant?

JOAN. My voices do not tell me to disobey the Church; but God must be served first.

CAUCHON. And you, and not the Church, are to be the judge?

JOAN. What other judgment can I judge by but my own?

THE ASSESSORS [*scandalized*]. Oh! [*They cannot find words.*]

CAUCHON. Out of your own mouth you have condemned yourself. We have striven for your salvation to the verge of sinning ourselves: we have opened the door to you again and again; and you have shut it in our faces and in the face of God. Dare you pretend, after what you have said, that you are in a state of grace?

JOAN. If I am not, may God bring me to it: if I am, may God keep me in it!

Here I stand. I can do no other.
Martin Luther (1483–1546)

The Revolt Against the Church of Rome

Throughout medieval times, while the monks labored in their monastery workrooms to write down and pass on the words of the Bible and the teachings of the Church fathers, the Church itself grew rich and powerful. Popes and cardinals and bishops permitted those words to stay on the parchment on which they had been written, while they concerned themselves with increasing their wealth and power.

Pious men all over Europe began to be disturbed by the growing wealth and power of the Church. Some priests and monks preached and wrote against it. As early as 1300, Meister Eckhart, in Germany, fell into disfavor with Rome because of his preaching. In England, John Wyclif called for reforms and began the first translation of the Bible into English so that those without Latin might read it. In Holland, Geert Groote and Florentius Radewyn founded the Brothers of the Common Life in an effort to bring back the spirit of the primitive Church. John Huss went to his death in Bohemia because he exalted the importance of the individual conscience above the authority of any pope.

And then in Germany, about 1450, came one of the most important events in the history of the Western world for the relation of men to their faith. Johann Gutenberg printed the Bible, the first book to come from his newly invented press, and, for the first time, the Word of God became easily accessible to all who could read it. More and more men turned to the Bible, read it, and found many things in it which made the Church of their day seem unfaithful to its own teachings.

Even in Italy, voices were raised against the pope. Girolamo Savaranola, a Florentine monk, was burned at the stake for his preaching. Finally, with the appearance of Martin Luther in Germany, the revolt against the Church reached its peak. Luther's followers included many of the German princes and in 1529, when at the insistence of the Holy Roman Emperor the Diet of Speyer issued an edict against them and their religious practices, they protested strongly. From their protest, those who differed with Rome became known, from then on, as *Protestants*.

Similar movements began to gather followers in Switzerland, under John Calvin in Geneva and Ulrich Zwingli in Zurich. In England, Henry VIII's quarrel with the pope separated the English Church from Rome. And John Knox, in Scotland, freed the Church of his country from both Rome and England.

Most of what happened in this period is known as the Reformation, a movement of the spirit which really started much earlier and still continues. For us, however, what is important is that the Protestant churches we know today were first shaped in those times by the great men to whom this section of this book is devoted.

FROM THE SERMONS OF MEISTER ECKHART

I have a capacity in my soul for taking in God entirely. I am as sure as I live that nothing is so near to me as God. God is nearer to me than I am to myself; my existence depends of the nearness and presence of God.

In whichever soul God's Kingdom appeareth, and which knoweth God's Kingdom, that soul needeth no human preaching or instruction; it is taught from within and assured of eternal life.

As for outward works they are ordained for this purpose that the outward man may be directed to God. But the inner work, the work of God in the soul is the chief matter; when a man finds this within himself, he can let go externals. No law is given to the righteous, because he fulfills the law inwardly.

FROM THE WRITINGS OF JOHN WYCLIF

... they [the priests] attend more to wrongful commandments of sinful men than to the most rightful commandments of
God. For if the pope or bishop send a letter to receive a pardoner
to deceive the people, by grants of many thousand years of pardon, he shall be despatched; although if there come a true man, to
preach the gospel freely and truly, he shall be hindered for
wrongful command of a sinful man. And thus they put God's
commandment and his rightful will behind, and put sinful man's
will and wrong commandments before; and thus for their own
worldly profit and bodily ease they stop their parishioners from
hearing of God's law, which is food for the soul, and lead them
blindly to hell.

... they think more of statutes of sinful men than the most
reasonable law of Almighty God. For they dread the pope's law,
and statutes made by bishops, and other officers, more than the
noble law of the gospel. Therefore they have many great and
costly books of man's law, and study them much, but few curates
have the Bible and expositions of the gospel, they study them but
little and do them less. But would to God that every parish
church in this land had a good Bible and good expositions on
the gospel, and that the priests studies them well, and taught
truly the gospel and God's commands to the people!

THE FOLLOWERS OF WYCLIF

JOHN FISKE

The work which Wyclif had begun in the fourteenth century had continued to go on in spite of occasional spasmodic attempts to destroy it with the aid of the statute passed in 1401 for the burning of heretics.

The feature which characterized the Lollards [Wyclif's followers] in common was a bold spirit of inquiry which led them, in spite of persecution, to read Wyclif's English Bible and call in question such dogmas and rites of the church as did not seem to find warrant in the sacred text. Clad in long robes of coarse red wool, barefoot, with pilgrim's staff in hand, the Lollard preachers fared to and fro among the quaint Gothic towns and shaded hamlets, setting forth the word of God wherever they could find listeners, now in the parish church or under the vaulted roof of the cathedral, now in the churchyard or marketplace, or on some green hillside. During the fifteenth century persecution did much to check this open preaching, but passages from Wyclif's tracts and texts from the Bible were copied by hand and passed about among tradesmen and artisans, yeomen and ploughboys, to be pondered over and talked about and learned by heart. It was a new revelation to the English people, this discovery of the Bible. Christ and his disciples seemed to come very near when the beautiful story of the gospels was first read in the familiar speech of everyday life. Heretofore they might well have seemed remote and unreal, just as the schoolboy hardly realizes that the Cato and Cassius over whom he puzzles in his Latin lessons were once living men like his father and neighbors, and not mere nominatives

63

governing a verb, or ablatives of means or instrument. Now it became possible for the layman to contrast the pure teachings of Christ with the doctrines and demeanour of the priests and monks to whom the spiritual guidance of Englishmen had been entrusted. Strong and self-respecting men and women, accustomed to manage their own affairs, could not but be profoundly affected by the contrast.

While they were thus led more and more to appeal to the Bible as the divine standard of right living and right thinking, at the same time they found in the sacred volume the treasures of a most original and noble literature unrolled before them; stirring history and romantic legend, cosmical theories and priestly injunctions, profound metaphysics and pithy proverbs, psalms of unrivalled grandeur and pastorals of exquisite loveliness, parables fraught with solemn meaning, the mournful wisdom of the preacher, the exultant faith of the apostle, the matchless eloquence of Job and Isaiah, the apocalyptic ecstasy of St. John. At a time when there was as yet no English literature for the common people, this untold wealth of Hebrew literature was implanted in the English mind as in a virgin soil. Great consequences have flowed from the fact that the first truly popular literature in England—the first which stirred the hearts of all classes of people, and filled their minds with ideal pictures and their every-day speech with apt and telling phrases—was the literature comprised within the Bible.

FROM THE WORDS OF JOHN HUSS

So far as the mandates of the Roman pontiff are . . . according to the rule of Christ . . . so far I intend most certainly to obey them. But if I find them to be at variance, I will not obey them, even if you put before my eyes fire for the burning of my body.

. . . I withstood the bull of Alexander V, which Lord Zbynek, Archbishop of Prague, secured, 1409, and in which he commands that there should be no more preaching of sermons to the people by any priest whatsoever—even though he might be fortified with an apostolic instrument taking precedence of such a mandate or by any other written instrument—except in cathedrals, parochial or cloistral churches, or in their cemeteries. This mandate, being contrary to the words and deeds of Christ and his apostles, is not apostolic, for Christ preached to the people on the sea, in the desert, in the fields and houses, in synagogues, in villages and on the streets, and taught his disciples, saying: "Go ye into all the world and preach the Gospel to every creature," Mark 16:15. And these, going forth, preached everywhere, that is, in every place where the people were willing to listen, God working with them. Therefore, this command is to the hurt of the church, and binds the Word of God, that it should not run freely.

THE EXECUTION OF JOHN HUSS OF BOHEMIA

PHILIP SCHAFF

It was midday. The prisoner's hands were fastened behind his back, and his neck bound to the stake by a chain. On the same spot some time before, so the chronicler notes, a cardinal's worn-out mule had been buried. The straw and wood were heaped up around Huss' body to the chin, and rosin sprinkled upon them. The offer of life was renewed if he would recant. He refused and said, "I shall die with joy today in the faith of the Gospel which I have preached." When Richental, who was standing by, suggested a confessor, he replied, "There is no need of one. I have no mortal sin." At the call of bystanders, they turned his face away from the East, and as the flames arose, he sang twice, Christ, thou Son of the living God, have mercy upon me. The wind blew the fire into the martyr's face, and his voice was hushed. He died, praying and singing.

A MIGHTY MAN

THOMAS CARLYLE

. . . no Time need have gone to ruin, could it have *found* a man great enough, a man wise and good enough: wisdom to discern truly what the Time wanted, valour to lead it on the right road thither; these are the salvation of any Time. But I liken common languid Times, with their unbelief, distress, perplexity, with their languid doubting characters and embarrassed circumstances, impotently crumbling down into ever worse distress towards final ruin;—all this I liken to dry dead fuel, waiting for the lightning out of Heaven that shall kindle it. The great man, with his free force direct out of God's own hand, is the lightning. His word is the wise healing word which all can believe in. All blazes round him now, when he has once struck on it, into fire like his own.

In all epochs of the world's history, we shall find the Great Man to have been the indispensable saviour of his epoch;—the light-ning, without which the fuel never would have burnt.

Luther's birthplace was Eisleben in Saxony; he came into the world there on the 10th of November 1483. It was an accident that gave this honour to Eisleben. His parents, poor mine laborers in a village of that region, named Mohra, had gone to the Eisleben Winter-Fair; in the tumult of this scene the Frau Luther was taken with travail, found refuge in some poor house there, and the boy she bore was named MARTIN LUTHER. Strange enough to reflect upon it. This poor Frau Luther, she had gone with her husband to make her small merchandisings; perhaps to sell the lock of yarn she had been spinning, to buy the small winter-necessaries for her narrow hut or household; in the whole world, that day, there was not a more entirely unimportant-looking pair of people than this Miner and his Wife. And yet what were all Emperors, Popes and Potentates, in comparison? There was born here, once more, a Mighty Man; whose light was to flame as the beacon over long centuries and epochs of the world; the whole world and its history was waiting for this man.

MARTIN LUTHER

WALTER RUSSELL BOWIE

Martin Luther began as a disciplined monk, devoted to his monastic order and obedient to the pope at Rome. But he became shocked at what he believed to be corruptions of faith and practice which were creeping into the Church, especially the sale for money of indulgences, which were promises in the name of the pope that, with proper payment, the buyer could be assured that there would be a shortening of the pains of purgatory after death. Luther dared to say that the pope had no power over purgatory; that popes had been in error and could be in error again, and that he, Martin Luther, could appeal to an authority of the Bible greater than the authority of the pope. By the direct mercy of Christ, and not through the machinery of the mass or through indulgences, the sinner could be redeemed. This challenged the claim of the Roman Church to hold the keys of heaven and hell.

Rome could not permit that sort of defiance. The pope forbade Luther to teach or preach. Then, when Luther refused to yield, there came one of the supremely dramatic scenes of history. Charles V, sovereign of the ancient and still awesome authority called the Holy Roman Empire, summoned the princes and nobles, the bishops and archbishops of Germany to meet in Imperial Diet in the city of Worms. Luther was ordered to appear for judgment. He was under condemnation by the pope, and the emperor was hostile. If he went to Worms, it would be at peril of his life.

Nevertheless, he went. When he approached the city, a great crowd swarmed out to meet him. The common people had little use for emperor or pope, and they saw in Luther a champion; but he knew that the heavy odds were on the other side. On his way to the palace where the Diet was assembled, an illustrious old soldier, General Frundsberg, clapped him on the shoulder, and said to him, "My poor monk! My little monk! Thou art on thy way to make a stand such as I and many of my knights have never done in our hardest battles!"

As Luther entered the crowded audience hall, Alexander, the papal legate, looked closely at him, and said afterward, "The fool entered smiling; he looked slowly round, and his face sobered." There was reason to be sober; for in that glittering assembly with its background of banners were gathered the might and majesty of medieval church and state.

On a table were Luther's books. He was asked if he would admit that they were his? Yes, he would admit it. Then came the question, "Do you wish to retract and recall them and their contents; or do you mean to adhere to them and to reassert them?"

Luther asked for time to deliberate, "that I may answer the question without injury to the Word of God and without peril to my own soul."

Grudgingly, the emperor allowed the Diet to adjourn until the next day; then it reassembled. Now Luther would have the chance he had coveted to make his full defense. He reviewed the books that lay before him and the truths of the gospel which he believed them to obtain. To that gospel he appealed, and to the free soul's reception of it. As to what he had written, "Confute me," he concluded, "by proofs of Scripture, or else by plain, just arguments: I cannot recant otherwise. For it is neither safe nor prudent to do aught against conscience. Here stand I; I can do no other: God assist me!"

Thus he stood, in his monk's robe and cowl, alone and seemingly unbefriended. Yet he was not altogether without friends, even in that august assembly which stared at him in what seemed ominous, grim silence.

Charles V, as well as the papal legate, was outraged. Here was this presumptuous monk exalting his individual conscience above the divinely given authority of emperor and pope. But there were others who were ready to see that authority challenged, and they were on Luther's side because he dared to challenge it. Princes of Germany had read Luther's summons, *To the Christian Nobility of the German Nation*, his *Liberty of a Christian Man*, and his scathing arraignment of the papacy, *On the Babylonian Captivity of the Church*.

So while Spaniards in the Diet shouted that Luther should be condemned as a heretic, German knights ringed round and escorted him from the hall.

A MIGHTY FORTRESS IS OUR GOD

MARTIN LUTHER

A mighty fortress is our God,
  A bulwark never failing;
Our helper he amid the flood
  Of mortal ills prevailing:
For still out ancient foe
Doth seek to work us woe;
His craft and power are great,
And, armed with cruel hate,
  On earth is not his equal.

Did we in our own strength confide,
  Our striving would be losing;
Were not the right man on our side,
  The man of God's own choosing:
Dost ask who that may be?
Christ Jesus, it is he;
Lord Sabaoth his Name,
From age to age the same.
  And he must win the battle.

And though this world, with devils filled,
  Should threaten to undo us;
We will not fear, for God hath willed
  His truth to triumph through us:
The prince of darkness grim,
We tremble not for him;

His rage we can endure,
For lo! his doom is sure,
   One little word shall fell him.

That word above all earthly powers,
   No thanks to them, abideth;
The spirit and the gifts are ours
   Through him who with us sideth:
Let goods and kindred go,
This mortal life also;
The body they may kill:
God's truth abideth still,
   His kingdom is for ever.

FROM THE WORDS OF MARTIN LUTHER

The Christian Church keeps all words of God in its heart, and turns them round and round, and keeps their connection with one another and with Scripture! Therefore, anyone who is to find Christ must first find the Church. How could anyone know where Christ is and faith in Him is, unless he knew where His believers are? Whoever wishes to know something about Christ must not trust to himself, nor by the help of his own reason build a bridge of his own to heaven, but must go to the Church, must visit it and make inquiry. Now the Church is not wood and stone, but the company of people who believe in Christ. With these he must unite and see how they believe, live, and teach, who assuredly have Christ among them. For outside the Christian Church there is no truth, no Christ, no blessedness.

. . . the business of the true apostle is to preach Christ's passion, resurrection, and saving office, and to lay the foundation on which others may stand with him—just as Christ said: 'You shall be my witness' (John 15:27). And here is the essential agreement of all the authentic holy books, that together they preach Christ and call men to Him. This is also the proper criterion for criticizing any book. Look to see if it calls men to Christ or not, since all Scripture testifies of Christ (Romans 3:21) and St. Paul will know nothing but Christ (I Cor. 2:2). What does not teach Christ is not apostolic even if St. Peter or St. Paul were doing the teaching. On the other hand, whatever preaches Christ is apostolic even if Judas, Annas, Pilate, or Herod were doing the preaching.

Faith is the one demand of God. But this faith is no mere matter of beliefs or acceptance of the Church's teaching. It is a self-surrendering trust in a Person—in Christ as God's word of mercy and as God's will for us. It is no single act but a constant and continuing attitude, in which a man gives himself in utter obedience to God while at the same time he lives in trustful dependence on God. Faith, then, does not need morality as a supplement of good works, because it already includes this. Out of it there flows forth the whole Christian life as God desires it— the life of sons in the freedom of faith, the life of service in the obedience of love.

A Christian man is a most free lord of all things and subject to no one; a Christian man is a most dutiful servant of all things and subject to everyone.

Every Christian is by faith so exalted above all things that in spiritual power he is completely lord of all. Nothing whatever can do him any hurt, but all things are subject to him and are compelled to be subservient to his salvation. . . . This is a spiritual power ruling in the midst of enemies and mighty in the midst of distresses. And it is nothing else than that strength is made perfect in weakness, and in all things I am able to gain salvation, so that even the cross and death are compelled to serve me and work together for salvation. For this is a high and illustrious dignity, a true and almighty power, a spiritual empire, in which there is nothing so good, nothing so bad as not to work together for my good if only I believe. . . . A Christian man needs no work, no law for salvation, for by faith he is free from all law and in perfect freedom does gratuitously all he does, seeking neither profit nor salvation, but only what is well-pleasing to God, since by the grace of God he is already satisfied and saved through his faith.

What you do in your house is worth as much as if you did it up in Heaven for our Lord God. For what we do in our calling here on earth in accordance with His word and command He counts as if it were done in heaven for Him. . . . In whatever calling God has placed you, do not abandon it when you become a Christian. If you are a servant, a maid, a workman, a master, a housewife, a mayor, a prince, do whatever your position demands. For it does not interfere with your Christian faith and you can serve God rightly in any vocation. . . . Therefore we should accustom ourselves to think of our position and work as sacred and well-pleasing to God, not on its own account, but because of the word and the faith from which our obedience flows. No Christian should despise his position if he is living in accordance with the word of God, but should say, "I believe in Jesus Christ, and do as the ten commandments teach, and pray that our dear Lord God may help me thus to do." That is a right holy life, and cannot be made holier even if one fast oneself to death. . . . It looks like a great thing when a monk renounces everything, goes into a cloister, lives a life of asceticism, fasts, watches, prays and the like. Works in abundance are there. But God's command is lacking, and so they cannot be gloried in as if done for Him. On the other hand it looks like a small thing when a maid cooks, and cleans, and does other housework. But because God's command is there, even such a lowly employment must be praised as a service of God, far surpassing the holiness and asceticism of all monks and nuns. Here there is no command of God. But there God's command is fulfilled, that one should honor Father and Mother and help in the care of the home.

JOHN CALVIN

WALTER RUSSELL BOWIE

The message of the Reformation came into France also. But the followers of the pope, who now were called the Catholics, hunted down the Protestants wherever they were found.

From a Catholic family of France came a man who was to rank with Luther and Zwingli as one of the great reformers— though most of his life, and his death, would be outside his own country. His name was John Calvin.

In his youth Calvin was on the way to becoming a priest. Then he began to study law. At the universities of Paris and Orléans he was such a brilliant scholar that he was called on to lecture if the regular professors were away. Meanwhile he was learning Greek and reading the New Testament. Also he was beginning to read the writings of Luther that had been brought, at the risk of those who dared to have them, into France.

Like the humanists and other men who were not afraid to think, Calvin already saw that there were many abuses that needed to be corrected in the Church. But now he became convinced of more than that. Luther was right. There had to be a whole new understanding of the gospel, based directly on the New Testament and not on the partly corrupted practices of the Church of Rome.

Soon therefore Calvin joined one of the little groups of Protestants that were secretly growing in France. Twice he was arrested and briefly imprisoned. Switzerland was being torn by religious war, but some parts of it at least seemed safer than France. Calvin made his way to the city of Basle. What he wanted to do was to settle down in quiet to study and to write. And he did write. When he was only twenty-six years old, he

77

published the book that has put its mark on Protestant thought more than almost any other book ever written, his *Institutes of the Christian Religion*.

On a journey Calvin had to stop in Geneva. There to his inn came an overpowering visitor. This was William Farel, who was already preaching the reformed gospel in the city. Farel was a man of burning conviction, with a tremendous voice. Once when he was preaching in a church, Roman Catholic opponents set all the tower bells ringing; but Farel made a great crowd hear him through all the din of the bells. Now he besieged Calvin with passionate argument. Calvin's duty, Farel said, was to leave Basle and come to work in Geneva. Farel made Calvin feel that not to listen might be a dreadful sin of disobedience. Calvin said afterward that it was "as if God had stretched forth his hand upon me from on high to arrest me."

So Calvin did come to Geneva, and he and Farel worked together. Now there was to be an end to the quiet that Calvin had longed for. The city council that governed Geneva had voted to allow no more authority of Rome. The Reformation gospel could be preached in the churches. But that did not mean that all the people were ready yet for a new kind of Christian life. They were ready to get rid of sellers of indulgences and of having money go out of Switzerland to Rome. But this did not make them welcome preachers who wanted to reform their morals. Geneva was a turbulent city with plenty of drunkenness, gambling, and loose living generally.

It was not long before rioting broke out against Farel and Calvin. They were preaching in plain words about the sins that people had to stop committing if they were to come to church. There was one man whose evil living was so notorious that Farel and Calvin gave notice that they would forbid his coming to Communion. On an Easter Sunday he was there. An angry, crowded congregation watched to see what would happen. Calvin stood up and announced that if any unworthy person dared to try to come to the Communion, there would be no Communion for anyone. And there was none. He closed the service.

Calvin and Farel were followed through the streets with

threats and curses. The city council met and banished them from Geneva.

But conditions in Geneva went from bad to worse, and people began to change their minds. After three years they appealed to Calvin to come back. So he returned, though Farel, who was working in another city, would not be with him again.

For the rest of his life, until he died worn out by labors in which he never spared himself, Calvin made Geneva a Reformation stronghold. Protestants persecuted in other lands fled there for refuge, and preachers went out from it to carry the beliefs they had heard preached and seen practiced in Geneva.

Religion was no empty form or easy word for Calvin. He wanted all Geneva to live seven days a week according to what he believed to be God's commandments. He started schools where children would be taught the catechism which he wrote for them. He wanted the laws of the Church to determine the laws of the city. Every congregation was governed by its elected elders; and the elders met together in an assembly called the presbytery, which made the rules for the whole Church. Thus arose the name Presbyterian for those Christian churches in many countries that trace their history back to Geneva and to Calvin.

Geneva was on the border of France, and France was still fiercely Roman Catholic. So were parts of Switzerland. Calvin believed that if the Church in Geneva was to live, it had to be disciplined like an army of the Lord. Its people must be like the Israelites in Old Testament times when they were on guard against the Canaanites and the Midianites and other enemies round about. The people of the Reformation were the new chosen people, inheritors of the promise God had made to Abraham. And if they were to deserve his promise, they must completely obey his law.

Therefore Calvin tried to order life in Geneva according to what he thought was the pattern of holiness. There were stern punishments not only for the wicked but also for the careless and the easygoing. A man could be fined or imprisoned for playing dice for a bottle of wine or for laughing in church or going to sleep during a sermon, for doing anything he was not supposed

79

to do on the Sabbath or for wearing more showy clothes than were allowed.

It was a grim and stern kind of obedience that Calvin required. It could not be kept up for long. But in a time of danger it created men who had convictions and a courage that nothing could shake. From Calvin's teaching they believed in a God whose will is sovereign and whose purpose nothing can resist. They had no fear except the fear of being disobedient. And when they had set themselves to be faithful to what they thought was the will of God, they were not afraid of the face of any man.

THE RUDE TRUMPET

HENRY R. MAHLER, JR.

The Scottish peasant John Knox
entered the priesthood orthodox,
but the shocked echoes from Patrick Hamilton's burning
and the winds of heresy blowing free from across the sea
infected the Haddington notary-priest
till we find him on guard with a two-handed sword
while good George Wishart stood preaching the Word.
Soon Wishart, too, was burned at the stake,
and the reek of his burning drifting over moor and glen
did its work,
and sowed across Scotland the seeds of the reformed Kirk.

Gray St. Andrews by the cold north sea,
beleaguered in siege but religiously free,
offered its pulpit to the burgeoning Knox,
but soon the rude trumpet blowing its first hesitant sound
was throttled in silence as the French took the town.

Nineteen months as a galley slave
gave John Knox his maturation:
and the rhythm of the oars paced the "sobbes of his harte";
as his body hardened, his spirit hardened;
as his muscles knotted, his mind firmed;
and the iron entered his will;
and the fear of God drove out all fear of man.

Exile:
  in Berwick,

81

in Newcastle,
in Frankfurt,
in Geneva,
ten years of foreign apprenticeship
till the "Lords of the Congregation" summoned him back across
    the miles,
and by July of 1559 he was in Edinburgh, thundering
from the premier pulpit of the Church of St. Giles.

Beautiful Mary, Queen of the Scots,
ascended the throne and unflinchingly stood
on the right to say mass in Holyrood.
Notably unbewitched by the bewitching Queen,
John Knox, unmoved by her tantrums or tears,
solemnly lectured the frustrated lass
on the God-imposed duties attending a throne,
while the vacillating nobles maneuvered between
the unyielding Reformer and the lovely young Queen.

When a leader of men is disciplined, devout,
and the opponent is frivolous, irresponsible, vain,
the ultimate outcome is seldom in doubt.

John Knox bade fair to "ding his pulpit into blads,"
and in one hour put more life into his congregation
than five hundred trumpets,
and fought spiritual wickedness in high places,
till lying at last on his deathbed
he ordered the Scriptures incessantly read.

But the Kirk was alive and growing,
for unruly Scotland had heard
in a rude age
a rude trumpet blowing.

I will not cease from mental fight,
   Nor shall my sword sleep in my
   hand,
Till we have built Jerusalem
  In England's green and pleasant land.
        William Blake (1757–1827)

The English Contribution

The growth of Protestantism in America was, in the early days, a reflection of what was taking place in England. Although Scotland, Germany, Holland, and Sweden also sent Protestant settlers to the New World, the settlers from England dominated colonial America, and the churches they built reflected what was happening back home.

The Reformation in England began when the writings of Martin Luther, secretly brought in and distributed, spread his teachings. When this literature was found by church or state authorities, it was seized and burned. Then, in 1526, William Tyndale translated and had printed his English version of the New Testament, so that for the first time the common people could read the Scriptures for themselves. Although, ten years later, Tyndale was tracked down, arrested, strangled, and his body burned at the stake, the new religious ferment in England could not be suppressed.

There was increasing protest against many aspects of the

medieval church and especially against the oppressive control over thought and conscience represented by the papacy. A personal quarrel of Henry VIII with the pope coincided with a spreading desire for reform and for religious freedom. In 1534, the assemblies of the clergy in the north and south provinces, the Convocations of York and Canterbury, declared that "the bishop of Rome hath not by Scripture any greater authority in England than any other foreign bishop." Under Henry and his son, Edward VI, a series of reforms took place, the most important of which was putting the language of worship into that of the people—English.

Henry's daughter Mary followed Edward to the throne. Bitterly hostile to the Reformation, she arrested and executed the Archbishop and other leaders and attempted to return control of the Church of England to Rome, earning in the process the name of "Bloody Mary." Her reign was short and she was succeeded by her sister, Elizabeth I, who restored the English Book of Common Prayer and made final the separation of the Church of England from Rome.

In the years that followed, two influences strove for power in England. One was conservative and wanted to preserve the old forms, not too different except for language from the Church as it had been under Rome. The other, more radical, wanted to follow the continuing spirit of freedom and reform which Luther had symbolized in Germany. Complicated by domestic and foreign political factors, a long series of struggles began. Mary, Queen of Scots, attempted to overthrow Elizabeth. She failed and was executed. But when Elizabeth died in 1603, James Stuart, Mary's son, succeeded to the throne of England, to which Scotland was now united. For most of the seventeenth century, there was increasingly bitter conflict between James I and his descendants on the one side, and the protesting spirit of the Puritan party on the other. Finally, in 1688, the last of the Stuart kings, James II, who had become a Roman Catholic, was driven from England, and a new and soundly Protestant family was imported from Holland. With the coming of William and Mary, an act of Parliament required that the sovereign be a member of the Church of England. So the Anglican Church, which was to be the mother of the Protestant Episcopal Church in America, was firmly established in England.

But men continued to question the doctrines of the Church of England, and the new "dissenting" churches were established. As a result, although the first settlers from England to come to America brought the Church of England with them, those who followed, Puritans, Pilgrims, Quakers, and others, founded new churches based on their own doctrines.

Thus, when we look at Protestantism in England, we see two streams, two traditions. The first is that of the Established Church, so called because it is established by law as the Church of England. The second is that of the Dissenters, from which such churches as the Wesleyan, Methodist, and Baptist stem. In the pages that follow, both of these great traditions are represented because both have contributed to the shaping of Protestantism in America.

AN ENGLISH BIBLE

MARCUS L. LOANE

William Tyndale was born some time between the years 1490 and 1495, little more than a century after the death of John Wyclif. The facts of his early life are shrouded in the mists of uncertainty, but Foxe tells us that he was born "about the borders of Wales"; and it would seem that the Cotswolds and the Severn were the playground of his boyhood. He sprang from a house of yeoman farmers, and his kinsfolk were men of good standing in the Western Counties. His father and mother are quite unknown to the annals which have come down to us, but each of his brothers, John and Edward, was to feel the spiritual magnetism of the Reformation literature. No records now remain of his schooldays or the kind of education which he must have received, but there is one suggestive allusion in his own works which still deserves mention: "Except my memory fail me, and that I have forgotten what I read when I was a child, thou shalt find in the English Chronicle how that King Athelstane caused the Holy Scripture to be translated into the tongue that then was in England." He seems to have confused Athelstane with Alfred, but the recollection is a valuable sidelight on his boyhood. It is our one glimpse of the lad, evidently fond of reading, storing his mind with such items of history, artlessly disclosing his life's master passion. But he grew up in a county where he would see the Church at the lowest ebb of spiritual vitality, for each parish priest did that which was right in his own eyes. The County of Gloucester was the most neglected Archdeaconry in the most neglected Diocese in all England. It was still part of the See of Worcester which had been farmed out to foreign prelates who had never so much as set foot in the realm, and which could boast

86

six mitred abbots who held seats in the House of Lords. But the common clergy were bogged in a mire of superstition which was nowhere surpassed in the length and breadth of England. "God it knoweth," wrote Tyndale, with regard to the priests of his own county, "there are a full ignorant sort, which have seen no more Latin than they read in their portresses and missals."

But the tale of appalling ignorance on the borders of Wales was just the worst of a series of tales which could be told of clergy throughout the realm. Thus in 1530, Tyndale himself bluntly affirmed that there were some twenty thousand priests in England, who could not so much as translate a plain clause from the Pater Noster into simple English. The Convocation of Canterbury had refused to allow any man to translate any part of Scripture into the English tongue, and the Bible was an unknown book to priests and laymen alike. Knowledge of the Scriptures would have perished from the land but for the forbidden translations which the Lollards read in secret. But the tidal waves of common feeling had been sapping the walls of the medieval fortress of Church life for many a year, and the voice of protest was now growing in volume and in frequency. It might be true that the Lollard Movement had been suppressed, true too that the Wyclif Bible had been proscribed: but John Purvey had once preached in Bristol, and the Lollards had been strongly entrenched in the west of England. We can hardly doubt that distant echoes of that stirring movement would reach the ears of the youthful Tyndale in the Vale of Berkeley. They would perhaps touch the chords of reality in his own mind even in the days before he had become aware of God's purpose in life for him. But that forbidden purpose was at work in his heart as he pondered the zeal of a king like Alfred, or the struggle of men like the Lollards. It was slowly to take shape in the form of a resolution to turn the Book of books into the kind of speech which the common people could read and understand. This was the grand motive behind all that he sought to do; it ran through his life and work like a thread of gold. There was little perhaps in the English Reformation so fine as the deliberate forgetfulness of self and the entire consecration of life which he brought to this task for God.

Foxe tells us that Tyndale was "brought up from a child in the University of Oxford." The voice of an unvaried tradition claims that he was enrolled as a student in Magdalen Hall, and we may fix the date of his entry about the year 1505. Tyndale himself held no brief in favour of the course of study prescribed; a few trenchant lines were enough to sum up his protest against the method of training men for the Church. "In the Universities," he wrote, "they have ordained that no man shall look on the Scripture until he be noselled in heathen learning eight or nine years, and armed with false principles with which he is clean shut out of the understanding of the Scripture." Logic was the essence of Arts, and the course left no room for the study of the Scriptures. It was a course which might foster sharpness of wit and much mental agility, but which could impart no spiritual fire and no real reverence for the truth. Things were little better when men passed from Arts to Theology, for even in Theology, the true purpose of the Scriptures had been buried out of sight in dismal oblivion. "Theology," so said Erasmus, "once venerable and full of majesty, had become almost dumb, poor, and in rags." Yet there were signs that it would not always be so, signs that the dawn of a new day was not far off. A few English scholars such as Colet and Grocyn and Linacre had been to Italy and had brought back a good report of the Renaissance in art and culture. The New Learning had found a voice in the halls of Oxford in the last years of the fifteenth century, and the Greek and Latin Classics had been held up for the admiration of the younger students in place of the medieval Schoolmen. Thus in 1496, John Colet had given the first of his famous lectures on the Pauline Epistles. It was his great desire to let the text speak for itself and to avoid the trammels of tradition. This was a bold innovation, but for ten years it was maintained with far-reaching results in the study of the Scriptures.

He was ahead of most men in that age in his vision and his grasp of reality, for as yet the Reformation had not produced any vernacular version of the Scriptures. Such an undertaking would be quite as novel and at least as adventurous as the voyage of Sebastian Cabot from nearby Bristol in search of the unknown beyond the seas. But the idea took firm hold of his mind, and his leisure hours were absorbed in new fields of study. He knew that John Wyclif had based his work on the Latin Vulgate which had been drawn up by Jerome a thousand years before; but he saw quite plainly that his work must be based on the Greek text of the *Novum Instrumentum* of 1516 or the *Novum Testamentum* of 1519. He could hardly know that Martin Luther was even then engaged in the preparation of his German New Testament from the same text; but he was in fact to do for England just what Luther was doing for Germany. Foxe tells us that it was at this time that he fell into dispute with a certain man who boldly affirmed that men would be better without the laws of God than they would be without those of the pope. Tyndale's reply showed that the die had now been cast beyond recall. "I defy the Pope and all his laws," he said; "If God spare my life, ere many years pass, I will cause a boy that driveth the plough shall know more of the Scriptures than thou dost."

. . . he reached the sorrowful conclusion that he would have to leave his own country if that need were ever to be supplied. "I . . . understood at the last," he wrote, "not only that there was no room in my Lord of London's palace to translate the New Testament, but also that there was no place to do it in all England." The one alternative would be to go abroad as a voluntary exile, so that he could employ the free printing presses of the Reformed countries. Therefore in May 1524, he left his books in the home of Humphrey Monmouth and took ship for Hamburg, little knowing that he would never again set foot in England.

Hamburg was a bustling city, immersed in the trade and commerce which would pass through its docks as one of the leading ports of Germany. But it was no city for a man like Tyndale, who was in search of the leisure which his studies required. But his movements are lost in the mists of obscurity, and there are few enough facts to guide us. Foxe says that "he took his journey into the further parts of Germany, as into Saxony, where he had conference with Luther and other learned men in those quarters." It is almost certain that he settled down in Wittenberg and went on with his work in its congenial environment for some nine or ten months. He had none of the aids which now seem so essential for the work of translation; grammars and lexicons were still few in number, thin in content, difficult to get, expensive to buy. He had no choice in the matter of the text which he would employ; he was confined to the *Novum Instrumentum* which had been reprinted as the *Novum Testamentum* with an improved text in 1519 and again in 1522. He had to base his work upon this text, and he compared his English translation with the Latin translation by Erasmus; then he compared it with that of Jerome in the Latin Vulgate, and with that of Luther in the German vernacular. He had to learn German before he could consult Luther; he had no friend with whom he could discuss questions of idiom. But his work was complete within the year . . .

. . . six thousand copies of the English New Testament had been printed by the spring of 1526. There are but two copies of this book still extant, and they are in the form of an octavo production. There were only a few minor alterations in the text of the book, but it left out the long prologue and the glosses which had been part of the work at Cologne. It gave the plain text of Scripture, without note or comment, but there was a short and moving address to the reader at the close of the book. No doubt it was reduced from a quarto volume to an octavo production owing to the change of printers and the pressure of time. Tyndale had in fact lost time as well as money in the Cologne venture, and it was plain wisdom to print the text and get it off his hands at once before his foes could strike again. Thus the spring saw thousands of New Testaments on their way to England, smuggled through the Customs in bales of cloth, in sacks of flour, in barrels and cases of every kind. German merchants had built up a large trade in the prohibited literature of the Reformation, and their English agents had worked out a skillful system by means of which such books were sold in the country towns and in the Universities. Tyndale's New Testament did not want for buyers who were willing to risk discovery, and Foxe informs us that "it can not be spoken what a door of light they opened to the eyes of the whole English nation."

There are few more moving stories than the saga which tells how the books were smuggled into England in spite of the vigilant watch of bishops and magistrates. They were bought and sold in secret for months before they came under the eyes of the authorities. They were passed from hand to hand with loving caution by those who were eager for true reform. There was no name on the title page to disclose Tyndale's identity, and it won an instant welcome on the ground of its own merit. But as summer wore on, its wide circulation seems to have become known to the authorities, who then had to decide on their course of action. It was soon brought under Wolsey's notice, and he arranged a conclave of prelates in his London palace to determine their policy. Tunstall was more concerned than most of the bishops because London was the major field of distribution. Thus he urged a course of stringent prohibition, and the bishops agreed that all copies of the book should be seized and burnt.

Accordingly in October 1526, Tunstall ordered his arch-deacons to call in all copies of the *New Testament* within thirty days, on pain of excommunication and suspicion of heresy. He had resolved to make known his disapproval by one of those displays of which the age was so fond, and late in the same month or early in November, there was a huge bonfire at Paul's Cross in London. Tunstall preached a sermon in which Tyndale's work was denounced as replete with error and heresy; then the condemned book was flung into the flames and burnt to ashes. This was endorsed by the Archbishop of Canterbury who drew up a letter for the bishops of the province urging them to adopt the same course of action. But it had small effect. Tunstall's lament that the book was spreading in large numbers throughout his See is the best proof that the merchants had sold their wares successfully, and the spectacular conflagration at Paul's Cross could not check the flow of books for which there was such a ready market. There had been a pirate reprint of three thousand copies, carried out in Antwerp, and some of these copies were in England by the middle of that same November. But the printer was placed under arrest, and some hundreds of copies were destroyed before they could cross the Channel. But men were not to be lightly deterred when they could see easy profits, and at least four unauthorized reprints took place within the next few years. This meant that some thirteen thousand copies, or more, were thrown into circulation. We do not know how the authorities solved the problem of its undisclosed authorship, but by the close of the year it had been traced to Tyndale. He had by then added to his offense by the publication of his *Prologue to the Epistle to The Romans*, and they began to plot revenge. But he was not unacquainted with the trend of affairs at home, for the fame of Tunstall's doings at Paul's Cross had spread far and wide throughout Europe on the wings of rumor. "In burning the New Testament, they did none other thing than that I looked for," Tyndale observed; and clear foresight led him to add: "No more shall they do, if they burn me also."

THE EXECUTION OF ARCHBISHOP THOMAS CRANMER

JOHN FOX

"And now I come to the great thing which so much troubleth my conscience, more than any thing that ever I did or said in my whole life, and that is the setting abroad of a writing contrary to the truth; which now here I renounce and refuse, as things written with my hand contrary to the truth; which I thought in my heart, and written for fear of death, and to save my life, if it might be; and that is, all such bills and papers which I have written or signed with my hand since my degradation, wherein I have written many things untrue. And forasmuch as my hand hath offended, writing contrary to my heart, therefore my hand shall first be punished; for when I come to the fire, it shall be first burned.

"And as for the pope, I refuse him, as Christ's enemy and Antichrist, with all his false doctrine.

"And as for the sacrament, I believe as I have taught in my book against the Bishop of Winchester, which my book teacheth so true a doctrine of the sacrament, that it shall stand at the last day before the judgment of God, where the papistical doctrine contrary thereto shall be ashamed to show her face."

Here the standers-by were all astonished, marveled, and amazed. . . . some of them began to cry out, yelp, and bawl . . . "Stop the heretic's mouth, and take him away."

And then Cranmer, being pulled down from the stage, was led to the fire. . . .

But when he came to the place where the holy bishops and martyrs of God, Bishop Latimer and Bishop Ridley, were burnt

93

before him for the confession of the truth, kneeling down he prayed to God, and not long tarrying in his prayers, putting off his garment to his shirt, he prepared himself for death.

And when the wood was kindled, and the fire began to burn near him, he stretched forth his right hand, which had signed his recantation, into the flames, and there held it so steadfast that all the people might see it burnt to a coal before his body was touched. In short, he was so patient and constant in the midst of these extreme tortures, that he seemed to move no more than the stake to which he was bound; his eyes were lifted up to heaven, and often he repeated, "this unworthy right hand," so long as his voice would suffer him; and as often using the words of the blessed martyr St. Stephen, "Lord Jesus, receive my spirit," till the fury of the flames putting him to silence, he gave up the ghost.

A CANDLE FOR ENGLAND

JOHN FOX

On the accession of Queen Mary, he [Nicholas Ridley, Bishop of London] shared the same fate with many others who professed the truth of the gospel. Being accused of heresy, he was first removed from his bishopric, then sent prisoner to the Tower of London, and afterwards to Bocardo prison, in Oxford; from whence he was committed to the custody of Mr. Irish, mayor of that city, in whose house he remained till the day of his execution.

On the north side of the town, in the ditch over-against Balliol College, the place of execution was appointed: and for fear of any tumult that might arise to hinder the burning of the servants of Christ, the lord Williams was commanded by the queen's letters, and the householders of the city to be there assistant, sufficiently appointed; and when every thing was in readiness, the prisoners were brought forth by the mayor and bailiffs.

Dr. Ridley, then looking back, saw Mr. Latimer, coming after. Unto whom he said, 'Oh, are you there?'—'Yea,' said Mr. Latimer, 'have after, as fast as I can.' So he following a pretty way off, at length they came to the stake. Dr. Ridley first entering the place, earnestly held up both his hands, and looked towards heaven: then shortly after seeing Mr. Latimer with a cheerful look, he ran to him, and embraced him, saying, 'Be of good heart, brother, for God will either assuage the fury of the flame, or else strengthen us to abide it.'

He then went to the stake, and, kneeling down, prayed with great fervor, while Mr. Latimer following, kneeled also, and prayed as earnestly as he.

He then, with Mr. Latimer, kneeled to my lord Williams, the

95

vice-chancellor of Oxford, and the other commissioners appointed for that purpose, who sat upon a form thereby, and said, 'I beseech you, my lord, even for Christ's sake, that I may speak but two or three words:' and whilst my lord bent his head to the mayor and vice-chancellor, to know whether he might have leave to speak, the bailiffs, and Dr. Marshal, the vice-chancellor, ran hastily unto him, and with their hands stopping his mouth, said, 'Mr. Ridley, if you will revoke your erroneous opinions, you shall not only have liberty so to do; but also your life.'—'Not otherwise?' said Dr. Ridley.—'No,' answered Dr. Marshal. 'Therefore if you will not do so, there is no remedy: you must suffer for your deserts.'—'Well,' said the martyr, 'so long as the breath is in my body, I will never deny my Lord Christ, and his known truth: God's will be done in me.' With that he rose and said with a loud voice, 'I commit our cause to Almighty God, who will indifferently judge all.'

To which Mr. Latimer added his old saying, 'Well, there is nothing hid but it shall be opened;' and said he could answer Smith well enough, if he might be suffered. They were then commanded to prepare immediately for the stake.

They then brought a lighted fagot, and laid it at Dr. Ridley's feet; upon which Mr. Latimer said, 'Be of good comfort, Mr. Ridley, and play the man: we shall this day light such a candle by God's grace in England, as I trust never shall be put out.' When Dr. Ridley saw the fire flaming up towards him, he cried with an amazing loud voice: 'Into thy hands, O Lord, I commend my spirit; Lord, receive my spirit;' and continued often to repeat, 'Lord, Lord, receive my spirit.' Mr. Latimer, on the other side, cried as vehemently. "O father of heaven, receive my soul.'

FROM THE PILGRIM'S PROGRESS

JOHN BUNYAN

As I walked through the wilderness of this world, I lighted on a certain place where was a Den, and I laid me down in that place to sleep: and, as I slept, I dreamed a dream. I dreamed, and behold, I saw a man clothed with rags, standing in a certain place, with his face from his own house, a book in his hand, and a great burden upon his back (*Isa. lxiv. 6; Luke xiv. 33; Ps. xxxviii. 4; Hab. ii. 2*). I looked, and saw him open the book and read therein; and, as he read, he wept and trembled; and, not being able longer to contain, he brake out with a lamentable cry, saying. "What shall I do?" (*Acts ii. 37, xvi. 30, 31*).

Now, I saw, upon a time, when he was walking in the fields, that he was, as he was wont, reading in his book, and greatly distressed in his mind; and, as he read, he burst out, as he had done before, crying, "What shall I do to be saved?"

I saw also that he looked this way and that way, as if he would run; yet he stood still, because, as I perceived, he could not tell which way to go. I looked then, and saw a man named Evangelist coming to him, who asked, Wherefore dost thou cry?

He answered, Sir, I perceive by the book in my hand, that I am condemned to die, and after that to come to judgment (*Heb. ix. 27*); and I find that I am not willing to do the first (*Job xvi. 21*), nor able to do the second (*Ezek. xxii. 14*).

Christian no sooner leaves the World but meets
Evangelist, who lovingly him greets
With tidings of another; and doth show
Him how to mount to that from this below.

Then said Evangelist, If this be thy condition, why standest thou still? He answered, Because I know not whither to go. Then he gave him a parchment roll, and there was written within, "Flee from the wrath to come" (*Matt. iii. 7*).

The man therefore read it, and looking upon Evangelist very carefully, said, Whither must I fly? Then said Evangelist, pointing with his finger over a very wide field, Do you see yonder wicket-gate? (*Matt. vii. 13, 14*). The man said, No. Then said the other, Do you see yonder shining light? (*Ps. cxix. 105; 2 Pet. i. 19*). He said, I think I do. Then said Evangelist, Keep that light in your eye, and go up directly thereto: so shalt thou see the gate; at which, when thou knockest, it shall be told thee what thou shalt do.

Now, as Christian was walking solitarily by himself, he espied one afar off, come crossing over the field to meet him; and their hap was to meet just as they were crossing the way of each other. The gentleman's name that met him was Mr. Worldly Wiseman: he dwelt in the town of Carnal Policy, a very great town, and also hard-by from whence Christian came. This man, then, meeting with Christian, and having some inkling of him,—for Christian's setting forth from the City of Destruction was much noised abroad, not only in the town where he dwelt, but also it began to be the town-talk in some other places,—Mr. Worldly Wiseman, therefore, having some guess of him, by beholding his laborious going, by observing his sighs and groans, and the like, began thus to enter into some talk with Christian.

Worldly. How now, good fellow, whither away after this burdened manner?

Christian. A burdened manner, indeed, as ever, I think, poor creature had! And whereas you ask me, Whither away. I tell you, sir, I am going to yonder wicket-gate before me; for there as I am informed, I shall be put into a way to be rid of my heavy burden.

Worldly. Hast thou a wife and children?

Chrisitan. Yes; but I am so laden with this burden, that I can-

98

not take that pleasure in them as formerly; methinks I am as if I had none (*1 Cor. vii. 29*).

Worldly. Wilt thou hearken unto me if I give thee counsel?

Christian. If it be good, I will; for I stand in need of good counsel.

Worldly. I would advise thee, then, that thou with all speed get thyself rid of thy burden; for thou wilt never be settled in thy mind till then; nor canst thou enjoy the benefits of the blessing which God hath bestowed upon thee till then.

Christian. That is that which I seek for, even to be rid of this heavy burden; but get it off myself, I cannot; nor is there any man in our country that can take it off my shoulders; therefore am I going this way, as I told you, that I may be rid of my burden.

Worldly. Who bid thee go this way to be rid of thy burden?

Christian. A man that appeared to me to be a very great and honourable person; his name, as I remember, is Evangelist.

Worldly. I beshrew him for his counsel! there is not a more dangerous and troublesome way in the world than is that unto which he hath directed thee; and that thou shalt find, if thou wilt be ruled by his counsel. Thou hast met with something, as I perceive already; for I see the dirt of the Slough of Despond is upon thee; but that slough is the beginning of the sorrows that do attend those that go on in that way. Hear me, I am older than thou; thou art like to meet with, in the way which thou goest, wearisomeness painfulness, hunger, perils, nakedness, sword, lions, dragons, darkness, and, in a word, death, and what not! These things are certainly true, having been confirmed by many testimonies. And why should a man so carelessly cast away himself, by giving heed to a stranger?

Christian. Why, sir, this burden upon my back is more terrible to me than are all these things which you have mentioned; nay, methinks I care not what I meet with in the way, if so be I can also meet with deliverance from my burden.

Worldly. How camest thou by the burden at first?

Christian. By reading this book in my hand.

Worldly. I thought so; and it is happened unto thee as to other weak men, who, meddling with things too high for them, do suddenly fall into thy distractions; which distractions do not only unman men, as thine, I perceive, has done thee, but they run them upon desperate ventures to obtain they know not what.

Christian. I know what I would obtain; it is ease for my heavy burden.

Worldly. But why wilt thou seek for ease this way, seeing so many dangers attend it? especially since, hadst thou but patience to hear me, I could direct thee to the obtaining of what thou desirest, without the dangers that thou in this way wilt run thyself into; yea, and the remedy is at hand. Besides, I will add, that, instead of those dangers, thou shalt meet with much safety, friendship, and content.

Christian. Pray, sir, open this secret to me.

Worldly. Why, in yonder village—the village is named Morality—there dwells a gentleman whose name is Legality, a very judicious man, and a man of a very good name, that has skill to help men off with such burdens as thine are from their shoulders: yea, to my knowledge, he hath done a great deal of good this way; ay, and besides, he hath skill to cure those that are somewhat crazed in their wits with their burdens. To him, as I said, thou mayest go, and be helped presently. His house is not quite a mile from this place, and if he should not be at home himself, he hath a pretty young man to his son, whose name is Civility, that can do it (to speak on) as well as the old gentleman himself; there, I say, thou mayest be eased of thy burden; and if thou art not minded to go back to thy former habitation, as, indeed, I would not wish thee, thou mayest send for thy wife and children to thee to this village, where there are houses now stand empty, one of which thou mayest have at reasonable rates; provision is there also cheap and good; and that which will make thy life the more happy is, to be sure, there thou shalt live by honest neighbours, in credit and good fashion.

Now was Christian somewhat at a stand; but presently he concluded, If this be true, which this gentleman hath said, my wisest course is to take his advice; and with that he thus further spoke.

Christian. Sir, which is my way to this honest man's house?

Worldly. Do you see yonder hill?

Worldly. By that hill you must go, and the first house you come at is his.

So Christian turned out of his way to go to Mr. Legality's house for help; but, behold, when he was got now hard by the hill, it seemed so high, and also that side of it that was next the wayside did hang so much over, that Christian was afraid to venture farther, lest the hill should fall on his head; wherefore there he stood still, and wotted not what to do. Also his burden now seemed heavier to him than while he was in his way. There came also flashes of fire out of the hill, that made Christian afraid that he should be burned (*Ex. xix. 16, 18*). Here, therefore, he sweat and did quake for fear (*Heb. xii. 21*).

When Christians unto Carnal men give ear,
Out of their way did go, and pay for't dear;
For Master Worldly Wiseman can but show
A saint the way to bondage and to woe.

And now he began to be sorry that he had taken Mr. Worldly Wiseman's counsel. And with that he saw Evangelist coming to meet him; at the sight also of whom he began to blush for shame. So Evangelist drew nearer and nearer; and coming up to him, he looked upon him with a severe and dreadful countenance, and thus began to reason with Christian.

Evangelist. What dost thou here, Christian? said he: at which words Christian knew not what to answer; wherefore at present he stood speechless before him. Then said Evangelist further, Art not thou the man that I found crying without the walls of the City of Destruction?

Christian. Yes, dear sir, I am the man.

Evangelist. Did not I direct thee the way to the little wicket-gate?

Christian. Yes, dear sir, said Christian.

Evangelist. How is it, then, that thou art so quickly turned aside? for thou art now out of the way.

Christian. I met with a gentleman so soon as I had got over the Slough of Despond, who persuaded me that I might, in the village before me, find a man that could take off my burden.

Evangelist. What was he?

Christian. He looked like a gentleman, and talked much to me, and got me at last to yield; so I came hither: but when I beheld this hill, and how it hangs over the way, I suddenly made a stand lest it should fall on my head.

Evangelist. What said that gentleman to you?

Christian. Why, he asked me whither I was going? And I told him.

Evangelist. And what said he then?

Christian. He bid me with speed get rid of my burden; and I told him it was ease that I sought. And, said I, I am therefore going to yonder gate, to receive further direction how I may get to the place of deliverance. So he said that he would show me a better way, and short, not so attended with difficulties as the way, sir, that you set me in; which way, said he, will direct you to a gentleman's house that hath skill to take off these burdens, so I believed him, and turned out of that way into this, if haply I might be soon eased of my burden. But when I came to this place, and beheld things as they are, I stopped for fear (as I said) of danger: but I now know not what to do.

Evangelist. Then, said Evangelist, stand still a little, that I may show thee the words of God. So he stood trembling. Then said Evangelist, "See that ye refuse not him that speaketh. For if they escaped not who refused him that spake on earth, much more *shall not* we *escape*, if we turn away from him that *speaketh* from heaven" (*Heb. xii. 25*). He said, moreover, "Now the just shall live by faith: but if *any man* draw back, my soul shall have no pleasure in him" (*Heb. x. 38*). He also did thus apply them: Thou art the man that art running into this misery; thou hast begun to reject the counsel of the Most High, and to draw back thy foot from the way of peace, even almost to the hazarding of thy perdition.

Then Christian fell down at his foot as dead, crying, "Woe is me, for I am undone!" At the sight of which, Evangelist caught him by the right hand, saying, "All manner of sin and blasphemies shall be forgiven unto men" (*Matt. xii. 31; Mark iii. 28*); "Be not faithless, but believing" (*John xx. 27*). Then did Christian again a little revive, and stood up trembling, as at first, before Evangelist.

Then Evangelist proceeded, saying, Give more earnest heed to the things that I shall tell thee of. I will now show thee who it was that deluded thee, and who it was also to whom he sent thee.—The man that met thee is one Worldly Wiseman, and rightly is he so called; partly, because he savoureth only the doctrine of this world (*1 John iv. 5*), (therefore he always goes to the town of Morality to church): and partly because he loveth that doctrine best, for it saveth him best from the cross (*Gal. vi. 12*). And because he is of this carnal temper, therefore he seeketh to prevent my ways, though right. Now there are three things in this man's counsel that thou must utterly abhor.

1. His turning thee out of the way. 2. His labouring to render the cross odious to thee. And, 3. His setting thy feet in that way that leadeth unto the administration of death.

Now Christian looked for nothing but death, and began to cry out lamentably; even cursing the time in which he met with Mr. Worldly Wiseman; still calling himself a thousand fools for hearkening to his counsel: he also was greatly ashamed to think that this gentleman's arguments, flowing only from the flesh, should have the prevalency with him as to cause him to forsake the right way. This done, he applied himself again to Evangelist in words and sense as follow:—

Christian. Sir, what think you? Is there hope? May I now go back and go up to the wicket-gate? Shall I not be abandoned for this, and sent back from thence ashamed? I am sorry I have hearkened to this man's counsel. But may my sin be forgiven?

Evangelist. Then said Evangelist to him, Thy sin is very great, for by it thou hast committed two evils: thou hast forsaken the way that is good, to tread in forbidden paths; yet will the man at the gate receive thee, for he has good-will for men; only, said he, take heed that thou turn not aside again, "lest thou

103

perish from the way, when his wrath is kindled but a little"
(*Ps. ii. 12*). Then did Christian address himself to go back; and
Evangelist, after he had kissed him, gave him one smile, and bid
him God-speed. So he went on with haste, neither spake he to any
man by the way; nor, if any asked him, would he vouchsafe them
an answer. He went like one that was all the while treading on
forbidden ground, and could by no means think himself safe,
till again he was got into the way which he left to follow Mr.
Worldly Wiseman's counsel. So, in process of time, Christian got
up to the gate. Now, over the gate there was written, "Knock,
and it shall be opened unto you" (*Matt. vii. 8*).

> "He that will enter in must first without
> Stand knocking at the gate, nor need he doubt
> That is A KNOCKER but to enter in;
> For God can love him, and forgive his sin."

He knocked, therefore, more than once or twice, saying—

> "May I now enter here? Will he within
> Open to sorry me, though I have been
> An undeserving rebel? Then shall I
> Not fail to sing his lasting praise on high."

At last there came a grave person to the gate, named Good-
will, who asked who was there? and whence he came? and what
he would have?

Christian. Here is a poor burdened sinner. I come from the
City of Destruction, but am going to Mount Zion, that I may
be delivered from the wrath to come. I would therefore, sir,
since I am informed that by this gate is the way thither, know if
you are willing to let me in!

Good-will. I am willing with all my heart, said he; and with
that he opened the gate.

After this it was noised abroad, that Mr. Valiant-for-truth was
taken with a summons by the same post as the other; and had
this for a token that the summons was true, "That his pitcher
was broken at the fountain" (*Ecc. xii. 6*). When he understood
it, he called for his friends, and told them of it. Then, said he,
I am going to my Father's; and though with great difficulty I

am got hither, yet now I do not repent me of all the trouble I have been at to arrive where I am. My sword I give to him that shall succeed me in my pilgrimage, and my courage and skill to him that can get it. My marks and scars I carry with me, to be a witness for me, that I have fought His battles who now will be my rewarder. When the day that he must go hence was come, many accompanied him to the river side, into which as he went he said, "Death, where is thy sting?" And as he went down deeper, he said, "Grave, where is thy victory?" So he passed over, and all the trumpets sounded for him on the other side.

HYMN

JOHN BUNYAN

He who would valiant be
  'Gainst all disaster,
Let him in constancy
  Follow the Master.
There's no discouragement
Shall make him once relent
His first avowed intent
  To be a pilgrim.

Who so beset him round
  With dismal stories,
Do but themselves confound,
  His strength the more is.
No foes shall stay his might,
Though he with giants fight;
He will make good his right
  To be a pilgrim.

Since, Lord, thou dost defend
  Us with thy Spirit,
We know we at the end
  Shall life inherit.
Then fancies flee away!
I'll fear not what men say,
I'll labor night and day
  To be a pilgrim.

CONSTANCY

GEORGE HERBERT

Who is the honest man?
He that doth still and strongly good pursue,
To God, his neighbour, and himself most true:
   Whom neither force nor fawning can
Unpin, or wrench from giving all their due.

   Whose honesty is not
So loose or easy, that a ruffling wind
Can blow away, or glittering look it blind:
   Who rides his sure and even trot,
While the world now rides by, now lags behind.

   Who, when great trials come,
Nor seeks, nor shuns them; but doth calmly stay,
Till he the thing and the example weigh:
   All being brought into a sum,
What place or person calls for, he doth pay.

   Whom none can work or woo,
To use in any thing a trick or sleight;
For above all things he abhors deceit:
   His words and works and fashion too
All of a piece, and all are clear and straight.

   Who never melts or thaws
At close temptations: when the day is done,
His goodness sets not, but in dark can run;

The sun to others writeth laws,
And is their virtue; Virtue is his Sun.

    Who, when he is to treat
With sick folks, women, those whom passions sway,
Allows for that, and keeps his constant way:
    Whom others' faults do not defeat;
But though men fail him, yet his part doth play.

    Whom nothing can procure,
When the wide world runs bias, from his will
To writhe his limbs, and share, not mend the ill.
    This is the Marksman, safe and sure,
Who still is right, and prays to be so still.

THE PULLEY

GEORGE HERBERT

When God at first made man,
Having a glass of blessings standing by;
Let us (said he) pour on him all we can:
Let the world's riches, which dispersed lie,
   Contract into a span.

So strength first made a way;
Then beauty flow'd, then wisdom, honour, pleasure:
When almost all was out, God made a stay,
Perceiving that alone, of all his treasure,
   Rest in the bottom lay.

For if I should (said he)
Bestow this jewel also on my creature,
He would adore my gifts instead of me,
And rest in Nature, not the God of Nature:
   So both should losers be.

Yet let him keep the rest,
But keep them with repining restlessness:
Let him be rich and weary, that at least,
If goodness lead him not, yet weariness
   May toss him to my breast.

THE ELIXIR

GEORGE HERBERT

Teach me, my God and King,
  In all things thee to see,
And what I do in any thing,
  To do it as for thee:

Not rudely, as a beast,
  To run into an action;
But still to make thee prepossest,
  And give it his perfection.
        ****
All may of thee partake:
  Nothing can be so mean,
Which with his tincture (*for thy sake*)
  Will not grow bright and clean.

A servant with this clause
  Makes drudgery divine:
Who sweeps a room, as for thy laws,
  Makes that and th' action fine.

This is the famous stone
  That turneth all to gold:
For that which God doth touch and own
  Cannot for less be told.

FROM THE WRITINGS OF JOHN MILTON

As therefore the state of man now is; what wisdom can there be to choose, what continence to forbear without the knowledge of evil? He that can apprehend and consider vice with all her baits and seeming pleasures, and yet abstain, and yet distinguish, and yet prefer that which is truly better, he is the true warfaring Christian. I can not praise a fugitive and cloistered virtue, un-exercised and unbreathed, that never sallies out to seek her adversary, but slinks out of the race, where that immortal garland is to be run for, not without dust and heat.

To be still searching what we know not, by what we know, still closing up truth to truth as we find it . . . this is the golden rule in theology as well as in arithmetic, and makes up the best harmony in a church; not the forced and outward union of cold and neutral, and inwardly divided minds.

Though all the winds of doctrine were let loose to play upon the earth, so truth be in the field, we do injuriously by licensing and prohibiting to misdoubt her strength. Let her and falsehood grapple; who ever knew truth put to the worse, in a free and open encounter?

JOHN WESLEY

WALTER RUSSELL BOWIE

One night, May 25, 1738, John Wesley went to a meeting of the Moravian Brethren in Aldersgate Street, London; and there he listened to the reading of Luther's *Preface to the Epistle to the Romans.* In Wesley's own words is the account of what then swept over him—a sudden conviction so decisive that he could mark the instant at which his life seemed to begin anew. "About a quarter before nine," he wrote afterward in his journal, "while he (i.e., Luther, whose words were being read) was describing the change which God works in the heart through faith in Christ, I felt my heart strangely warmed. I felt I did trust in Christ alone, for salvation; and an assurance was given me that he had taken away *my* sins, even *mine*, and saved me from the law of sin and death."

As W. E. H. Lecky has written in *The History of England in the Eighteenth Century,* "It is scarcely an exaggeration to say that the scene which took place at that humble meeting in Aldersgate Street forms an epoch in English history." Because of it, John Wesley from that time on had a living gospel which he would carry out as fire to kindle what was too generally the dormant religious life of England.

In 1739, the year after his transforming experience in the Aldersgate Chapel, Wesley was invited by George Whitefield to come to Bristol and join in the unfettered evangelistic work which Whitefield has begun. He wrote in his *Journal:* "I could scarce reconcile myself at first to this strange way of preaching in the fields . . . having been all my life (till very lately) so tenacious of every point relating to decency and order, that I should have thought the saving of souls almost a sin, if it had not been done in a church." But he went, because he felt a "bounden duty," stronger than his inhibitions, "to declare unto all that are willing to hear, the glad tidings of salvation." And twenty years later, when he had preached to untold tens of thousands in fields, streets, market places and village squares, he wrote: "What marvel the devil does not love field preaching? Neither do I; I love a commodious room, a soft cushion, an handsome pulpit. But where is my zeal, if I do not trample all these under foot, in order to save one more soul?"

When Wesley had once launched upon his work of carrying the gospel to the unchurched crowds, the energy and the indomitable determination with which he pursued his purpose reached an ultimate of achievement which might have seemed beyond the strength of any human being. In eighteenth-century Britain, railroads had not been dreamed of. Travel was by horseback or by stage over roads that might be morasses of mud when heavy rains fell, or dangerous in winter from ice and drifted snow. Many rivers had no bridges and could be crossed only by uncertain ferries. But Wesley went not once but again and again through and across England and Scotland, from Kent and the coasts of Cornwall to the Scottish highlands; through Wales and Ireland, to London, Birmingham, Bristol, Liverpool, Dublin, and other great cities and villages past counting; to the Isle of Wight, the Isle of Man, and the Scilly and Channel Isles. For fifty-two years, in fair weather or foul, he rode five thousand to eight thousand miles a year, which added up to more than a quarter of a million miles in his lifetime; and he tells us that he discovered that his horse was never likely to stumble if he rode with a slack rein, which he always did, reading a book as he sat in his saddle. He preached fifteen times or more each week, and besides that, on the road or in the taverns where he stopped, he and any companion whom he took with him "were fully determined to lose no opportunity of awakening, instructing, or exhorting, any whom we might meet within our journey." It was hardly an exaggeration when Augustine Birrell called Wesley's *Journal*,

113

in which he set down what he had done, "the most amazing record of human exertion ever penned by man."

Wesley was often impatient with the well-to-do and the comfortable, who, he thought, were so padded with the soft satisfactions of their world that the sword of the Spirit could not touch them. But he had a passion of pity for the poor and the despised. He and the lay preachers whom he raised up as his helpers did more than any had ever done since the day of Francis of Assisi to bring the gospel to the common people. He knew that among the depraved—and all the more because of their depravity—there was a hidden hunger for the message of redemption which he brought. As he fed that hunger, human beings were transformed. "I have seen," he wrote, "(as far as a thing of this kind can be seen) very many persons changed in a moment from the spirit of fear, horror, despair, to the spirit of love, joy and peace, and from sinful desire till then reigning over them, to a pure desire of doing the will of God: him that was a drunkard and is now exemplarily sober: the whoremonger that was, who now abhors the very 'garment spotted by the flesh.' . . . This is the fact; let any judge of it as they please."

THE VILLAGE PARSON

OLIVER GOLDSMITH

Near yonder copse, where once the garden smiled,
And still where many a garden-flower grows wild;
There, where a few torn shrubs the place disclose,
The village preacher's modest mansion rose.
A man he was to all the country dear,
And passing rich with forty pounds a year;
Remote from towns he ran his godly race,
Nor e'er had changed, nor wished to change, his place,
Unskillful he to fawn, or seek for power,
By doctrines fashioned to the varying hour;
Far other aims his heart had learned to prize,
More skilled to raise the wretched than to rise.
His house was known to all the vagrant train,
He chid their wanderings but relieved their pain;
The long-remembered beggar was his guest,
Whose beard descending swept his aged breast;
The ruined spendthrift, now no longer proud,
Claimed kindred there, and had his claims allowed;
The broken soldier, kindly bade to stay,
Sat by the fire and talked the night away;
Wept o'er his wounds, or, tales of sorrow done,
Shouldered his crutch and showed how fields were won.
Pleased with his guests, the good man learned to glow,
And quite forgot their vices in their woe;

Careless their merits or their faults to scan,
His pity gave ere charity began.
    Thus to relieve the wretched was his pride,
And e'en his failings leaned to Virtue's side;
But in his duty prompt at every call,
He watched and wept, he prayed and felt for all.
And, as a bird each fond endearment tries
To tempt its new-fledged offspring to the skies,
He tried each art, reproved each dull delay,
Allured to brighter worlds, and led the way.

FROM THE COTTER'S SATURDAY NIGHT

ROBERT BURNS

The cheerfu' supper done, wi' serious face,
   They, round the ingle, form a circle wide;
The sire turns o'er, wi' patriarchal grace,
   The big ha' Bible, ance his father's pride;
   His bonnet rev'rently is laid aside,
His lyart haffets wearing thin an' bare;
   Those strains that once did sweet in Zion glide,
He wales a portion with judicious care;
And "Let us worship God!" he says, with solemn air.

Then kneeling down to Heaven's Eternal King,
   The saint, the father, and the husband prays:
Hope "springs exulting on triumphant wing,"
   That thus they all shall meet in future days;
   There ever bask in uncreated rays,
No more to sigh, or shed the bitter tear,
   Together hymning their Creator's praise,
In such society, yet still more dear;
While circling Time moves round in an eternal sphere.

Compared with this, how poor Religion's pride,
   In all the pomp of method, and of art,
When men display to congregations wide,
   Devotion's ev'ry grace, except the heart!
   The Power, incensed, the pageant will desert,
The pompous strain, the sacerdotal stole;
   But, haply, in some cottage far apart,
May hear, well pleased, the language of the soul:
And in His Book of life the inmates poor enroll.

ROCK OF AGES

A. M. TOPLADY

Rock of ages, cleft for me,
Let me hide myself in thee;
Let the water and the blood
From thy side, a healing flood,
Be of sin the double cure,
Cleanse me from its guilt and power.

Should my tears for ever flow,
Should my zeal no languor know,
All for sin could not atone:
Thou must save, and thou alone;
In my hand no price I bring,
Simply to thy cross I cling.

While I draw this fleeting breath,
When my eyelids close in death,
When I rise to worlds unknown
And behold thee on thy throne,
Rock of ages, cleft for me,
Let me hide myself in thee.

THOMAS CARLYLE

J. S. WHALE

Thomas Carlyle, the "Great Impatient" of the Victorian age, repudiated much of the Christian orthodoxy of his day and had some hard things to say of the Church and its preachers, even though the essential stuff of Scotland's Calvinism never ceased to smoulder, and sometimes to blaze, in his deepest being. Seated once with his ageing mother by her fireside at Ecclefechan, and inveighing against the preachers of his day, he exclaimed: "If I had to preach, I would go into the pulpit and say no more than this: 'All you people know what you ought to do; well, go and do it.'" His mother continued knitting in silence, and then replied: "Aye, Tammas; and will ye tell them how?"

SERMON AT RUGBY

THOMAS HUGHES

But what was it after all which seized and held these three hundred boys, dragging them out of themselves, willing or unwilling, for twenty minutes on Sunday afternoons? True, there always were boys scattered up and down the school, who, in heart and head, were worthy to hear and able to carry away the deepest and wisest words then spoken. But these were a minority always, generally a very small one, often so small a one as to be countable on the fingers of your hand. What was it that moved and held us, the rest of the three hundred reckless childish boys, who feared the Doctor with all our hearts, and very little besides in heaven or earth; who thought more of our sets in the school than of the church of Christ, and put the traditions of Rugby and the public opinion of boys in our daily life above the laws of God? We couldn't enter into half that we heard; we hadn't the knowledge of our own hearts or the knowledge of one another, and little enough of the faith, hope, and love needed to that end. But we listened, as all boys in their better moods will listen (aye, and man too for the matter of that), to a man who we felt to be with all his heart and soul and strength striving against whatever was mean and unmanly and unrighteous in our little world. It was not the cold clear voice of one giving advice and warning from serene heights, to those who were struggling and sinning below, but the warm living voice of one who was fighting for us and by our sides, and calling on us to help him and ourselves and one another. And so, wearily and little by little, but surely and steadily on the whole, was brought home to the young boy, for the first time, the meaning of his life: that it was no fool's or sluggard's paradise into which he had wandered by chance, but a battlefield, ordained from of old, where there are no spectators, but the youngest must take his side, and the stakes are life and death.

AN EXCERPT FROM RUGBY CHAPEL

MATTHEW ARNOLD

We were weary, and we
Fearful, and we in our march
Fain to drop down and to die.
Still thou turnedst, and still
Beckonedst the trembler, and still
Gavest the weary thy hand.
If, in the paths of the world,
Stones might have wounded thy feet,
Toil or dejection have tried
Thy spirit, of that we saw
Nothing: to us thou wast still
Cheerful, and helpful, and firm!
Therefore to thee it was given
Many to save with thyself;
And, at the end of thy day,
O faithful shepherd! to come,
Bringing thy sheep in thy hand.

Then, in such hour of need
Of your fainting, dispirited race,
Ye like angels appear,
Radiant with ardor divine.
Beacons of hope, ye appear!
Languor is not in your heart,
Weakness is not in your word,
Weariness not on your brow.
Ye alight in our van! at your voice,

Panic, despair flee away.
Ye move through the ranks, recall
The stragglers, refresh the outworn,
Praise, re-inspire the brave.
Order, courage, return;
Eyes rekindling, and prayers,
Follow your steps as ye go.
Ye fill up the gaps in our files,
Strengthen the wavering line,
Stablish, continue our march,
On, to the bound of the waste,
On, to the City of God.

MY MOTHER

J. M. BARRIE

For when you looked into my mother's eyes you knew, as if He had told you, why God sent her into the world—it was to open the minds of all who looked to beautiful thoughts.

She begins the day by the fireside with the New Testament in her hands, an old volume with its loose pages beautifully re-fixed, and its covers sewn and resewn by her, so that you would say it can never fall to pieces. It is mine now, and to me the black threads with which she stitched it are as part of the contents. Other books she read in the ordinary manner, but this one differently, her lips moving with each word as if she were reading aloud, and her face very solemn. The Testament lies open on her lap long after she has ceased to read, and the expression of her face has not changed.

So my mother and I go up the stairs together. "We have changed places," she says; "that was just how I used to help you up, but I'm the bairn now."

She brings out the Testament again; it was always lying within reach; it is the lock of hair she left me when she died. And when she has read for a long time she 'gives me a look,' as we say in the north, and I go out, to leave her alone with God. She had been but a child when her mother died, and so she fell early into the way of saying her prayers with no earthly listener. Often and often I have found her on her knees, but I always went softly away, closing the door. I never heard her pray, but I know very well how she prayed, and that, when that door was

123

shut, there was not a day in God's sight between the worn woman and the little child.

They knew now that she was dying. . . . then for some time she talked of the long lovely life that had been hers, and of Him to whom she owed it. She said good-bye to them all, and at last turned her face to the side where her best-beloved had lain, and for over an hour she prayed. They only caught the words now and again, and the last they heard were "God" and "love." I think God was smiling when He took her to Him, as He had so often smiled at her during those seventy-six years.

THE SECOND CRUCIFIXION

RICHARD LE GALLIENNE

Loud mockers in the roaring street
  Say Christ is crucified again:
Twice pierced his gospel-bearing feet,
  Twice broken his great heart in vain.

I hear and to myself I smile,
For Christ talks with me all the while.

No angel now to roll the stone
  From off his unawaking sleep,
In vain shall Mary watch alone,
  In vain the soldiers vigil keep.

Yet while they deem my Lord is dead
My eyes are on his shining head.

Ah! nevermore shall Mary hear
  That voice exceeding sweet and low
Within the garden calling clear:
  Her Lord is gone, and she must go.

Yet all the while my Lord I meet
In every London lane and street.

Poor Lazarus shall wait in vain,
  And Bartimeus still go blind;
The healing hem shall ne'er again
  Be touched by suffering mankind.

125

Yet all the while I see them rest,
The poor and outcast, on His breast.

No more unto the stubborn heart
  With gentle knocking shall he plead,
No more the mystic pity start,
  For Christ twice dead is dead indeed.

So in the street I hear men say,
Yet Christ is with me all the day.

IN MEMORIAM

ALFRED, LORD TENNYSON

Our little systems have their day;
   They have their day and cease to be:
   They are but broken lights of thee,
And thou, O Lord, art more than they.

We have but faith: we cannot know;
   For knowledge is of things we see;
   And yet we trust it comes from thee,
A beam in darkness: let it grow.

Let knowledge grow from more to more,
   But more of reverence in us dwell:
   That mind and soul, according well,
May make one music as before.

Our fathers' God, to Thee
Author of liberty,
  To Thee we sing;
Long may our land be bright
With Freedom's holy light;
Protect us by thy might,
  Great God, our King.
          Samuel Francis Smith (1808–95)

Diversity in America

After the discovery of America by Columbus in 1492, Catholic
Spain considered the Atlantic Ocean a private lake and the newly
discovered lands as hers forever. But the defeat of the Spanish
Armada by the English in 1588, during the reign of Elizabeth
I, opened the way for other settlements in the Americas. English
and Dutch Protestants, as well as French Catholics, quickly took
advantage of this.

Eventually, the English bested their Spanish, French, and
Dutch rivals and successfully colonized North America. And
it is from these first English colonies that the American Protestant tradition descends, although Protestant churches founded
by the Dutch still exist and prosper in the New York area. Later
on, Scandinavian and German Protestants made their contributions, first in Delaware and Pennsylvania and afterward in the
Midwest.

In Colonial America, as in England, the colonists were divided into the two great groups of English Protestantism, the Established Church, which became the Protestant Episcopal Church, and the Dissenters, who eventually formed the Baptist, Methodist, Presbyterian, Congregationalist, Quaker, Unitarian, and other churches.

The first permanent settlement in North America, at Jamestown, Virginia, also marked the beginnings of the Protestant Episcopal Church in America. As the conflict between Cromwell's Puritan reformers, the "Roundheads," and the adherents of the first Stuart kings, the "Cavaliers," turned into bloody warfare and the defeat of the Stuarts, increasing numbers of supporters of the Stuarts emigrated to Virginia and to the Carolinas, thus strengthening the Episcopal Church.

On the other hand, the Pilgrims and Puritans who settled New England and the Quakers who came to Pennsylvania were protesters against the doctrines and practices of the Church of England. In New England, the Puritans established their own church as the official church but, little more than 40 years after the *Mayflower* reached Provincetown, they were obliged to grant religious and political rights to others.

As the American settlers moved westward, opening up new areas, the influence of inherited religious forms diminished. Preachers were few and, on the frontier, Protestants welcomed ministers of any denomination. The Bible, in the King James Version, became the one common denominator of American Protestantism, although how it was interpreted often depended on just who was preaching.

Then, in the 18th century, America was stirred by a religious revival led by two great preachers, Jonathan Edwards and George Whitefield. Their meetings led to increased interest in religion but did not strengthen the existing churches. Instead, true to the tradition of dissent, many new sects arose to take members from other churches as well as from among the unchurched. Today, there are some 250 American Protestant denominations, with memberships ranging from in the millions to others whose numbers may be counted only in the hundreds.

The revivalist tradition in America continues, too, with such preachers as Billy Graham drawing enormous crowds from all denominations to his meetings.

The pages that follow demonstrate the variety and diversity of Protestantism in America.

PROPAGATING CHRISTIAN RELIGION

From the Jamestown Charter of 1606

James, by the Grace of God, King of England, Scotland, France, and Ireland, Defender of the Faith . . . our Licence, to make Habitation, Plantation, and to deduce a Colony of sundry of our People into that part of America, commonly called VIRGINIA . . .

We, greatly commending, and graciously accepting of, their Desires for the Furtherance of so noble a Work, which may, by the Providence of Almighty God, hereafter tend to the Glory of his Divine Majesty, in propagating of Christian Religion to such People, as yet live in Darkness and miserable Ignorance of the true Knowledge and Worship of God, and may in time bring the Infidels and Savages, living in those Parts, to human Civility, and to a settled and quiet Government . . .

THE PILGRIMS

DAVID LIVINGSTONE

The kingdom of God cometh not with observation. Luther simply followed the leadings of the Holy Spirit in the struggles of his own soul. He wrought out what the inward impulses of his own breast prompted him to work, and behold, before he was aware, he was in the midst of the Reformation. So, too, it was with the Plymouth pilgrims, with their sermons three times a day on board the *Mayflower*. Without thinking of founding an empire, they obeyed the sublime teachings of the Spirit, the promptings of duty and the spiritual life. God working mightily in the human heart is the spring of all abiding spiritual power; and it is only as men follow out the sublime promptings of the inward spiritual life, that they do great things for God.

LETTER FROM NEW ENGLAND

Words Carved on a Harvard Gate

"After God had carried us safe to New-England, and wee had builded our houses, provided necessities for our liveli-hood, rear'd convenient places for Gods worship, and settled the Civill Government; One of the next things we longed for, and looked after was to advance *Learning*, and perpetuate it to Posterity; dreading to leave an illiterate Ministry to the Churches, when our present Ministers shall lie in the Dust."

PURITANS

WILLIAM LYON PHELPS

I have been informed that some psychiatrists today urge parents not to teach their children the familiar prayer "Now I lay me down to sleep," because it will suggest to the infant mind

133

the thought of death and thus inspire fear at bedtime. The hard-boiled Puritan babies of New England got out of that prayer agreeable relaxation; they handed the responsibility over to God and went to sleep peacefully. I wonder what the psychiatrists would say to the verses my maternal grandmother, Mrs. Linsley, had for her mental furniture, for on the wall of a room in my house hangs a sampler, wrought by her little hands in 1790, when she was about five years old. It contains this cheerful poem:

> There is an hour when I must die,
> Nor do I know how soon 'twill come:
> A thousand children young as I,
> Are called by death to meet their doom.

The Puritans were determined not to let even children forget the certainty of death and the uncertainty of its hour. If they heard the laughter of children, they felt something ought to be done about it. And yet as carriers of gloom-germs, they were perhaps not so effective as our modern atheistical novelists. The Puritans felt that life was serious, but they had faith in the ultimate rightness of things; they believed this was God's world and that its darkness would be followed by eternal sunshine. Serious views of life seemed to them rational. But the modern pessimist, with no philosophy of life, and with no hope for humanity either here or hereafter, is as fully determined not to let us have any fun. The moment we try to enjoy ourselves we are called sternly to order. Now I cannot see that tears have any higher intellectual value than laughter; there may be as much cerebration in a comedy as in a tragedy. The Puritans believed that out of a dark soil bright flowers would spring; the modern pessimist offers us no flowers, but more dirt.

STEPHEN VINCENT BENÉT

Humility sat and sewed by her husband's side.
—Henry Shenton, come in the *Paragon*,
The butcher's lad with the white, impassioned face,
Older now but still with the mark on him
That shows the seeker, the man who is not content.
The babes were asleep but her husband was by her side
And he turned the leaves of a book, but she was content.

           He put down the book.
"Wife," he said, "when they come—the new colony—
And it seems they must—the men who come to the Bay—
Would it grieve you to leave this house?"
           "Aye, husband," she said,
Remembering deep in her youth the small, good place
And a father and mother talking while she listened,
Talking of voyages that were so far,
"Aye, it would grieve me somewhat, for the babes are young.
But if we must go, we must go."
           He ruffled his hair
In the one small boyish gesture that she loved.
"They are good men, here," he said in a solemn voice,
"And yet it is laid upon me to seek new ways.
I have kept my peace since we two were wed, Humility,
And yet I am not content on some points of grace.
I am not content. I have labored with Master Bradford
And he is full of the very spirit of God—
And yet, meseems, that he erreth; though, in the Hebrew,
It is also written—"

135

Her mouth and her face were grave
But she longed to say, "Dear heart, do I not know?
Dear heart that was kept in prison and fought the world
And so must ever seek for a thing unfound
And will not yield to the world, and yet is sweet.
You need not look so solemnly with your eyes,
For, without your eyes, I would know that we two must go.
And I am not strong as certain women are strong,
Yet I can bear more than they."
                        "They'll have books," he said,
"And I deem we may have much profitable discourse.
Nor may the things in my heart be always hid.
Have we fled England to live here under a rule,
And a dry rule, too—a dead and formal staff?
Nay, I'd speak of it to no other— but thou knowest—
The spirit works upon me and I must go."
"We will go," she said. "Now, am I not dutiful?"
And he stared at her for a moment and then he smiled
And, when he did, the face was boyish enough.

EDUCATION IN AMERICA

BENJAMIN RICE LACY, JR.

Just as political and economic life in the colonies was vitally influenced and indeed developed by Protestants, so also was education. It flourished in ratio to the Protestant spirit of the settlers. Time will not permit our tracing the effects of the teachings and disciplines of Luther and Melanchthon, Calvin and Zwingli and other Reformers, upon the universities and schools of Europe. They were often the centers of the Reformed Movement and one cannot think of Wittenberg without thinking of Luther, of Zurich without Zwingli, of Geneva without Calvin, of St. Andrews without Knox, of Oxford and Cambridge without Colet and Erasmus, Latimer and Ridley. The Genevan influence was so great that where Reformed or Presbyterian churches were planted in Holland, or in Great Britain, or in the New World, schoolhouses were hard by. The Puritans carried the first torch for education in the New World.

New England led all other sections both in point of time and in zeal for this cause. Harvard and Yale were founded under Puritan influence, and later Brown and Dartmouth succeeded them as the result of the religious impetus of the Great Awakening. The arrival and migration of the Scotch-Irish left a train of educational institutions wherever these people settled, beginning with the Log College in Pennsylvania and passing on to Nassau Hall, later Princeton University. We can follow their footsteps by the succession of academies which sprang up in Pennsylvania, Maryland, Virginia, the Carolinas, and Georgia.

The Protestant tradition demanded as educated citizenry, and the new republic which had been established under Protestant influence called for greater educational endeavors than could be accomplished by the churches separately. We can, therefore, say that public school education in America is largely the product of a Protestant civilization.

THE REVEREND MR. WHITEFIELD, PREACHER

BENJAMIN FRANKLIN

In 1739 arrived among us from Ireland the Reverend Mr. Whitefield, who had made himself remarkable there as an itinerant preacher. He was at first permitted to preach in some of our churches; but the clergy, taking a dislike to him, soon refused him their pulpits, and he was obliged to preach in the fields. The multitudes of all sects and denominations that attended his sermons were enormous, and it was a matter of speculation to me, who was one of the number, to observe the extraordinary influence of his oratory on his hearers, and how much they admired and respected him, notwithstanding his common abuse of them, by assuring them they were naturally *half beasts and half devils*. It was wonderful to see the change soon made in the manners of our inhabitants. From being thoughtless or indifferent about religion, it seemed as if all the world were growing religious, so that one could not walk through the town in an evening without hearing psalms sung in different families of every street.

And it being found inconvenient to assemble in the open air, subject to its inclemencies, the building of a house to meet in was no sooner proposed, and persons appointed to receive contributions, but sufficient sums were soon received to procure the ground and erect the building, which was one hundred feet long and seventy broad, about the size of Westminister Hall; and the work was carried on with such spirit as to be finished in a much shorter time than could have been expected. Both house and ground were vested in trustees, expressly for the use of any preacher of any religious persuasion who might desire to say something to the people at Philadelphia; the design in building not being to accommodate any particular sect, but the inhabitants in general; so that even if the Mufti of Constantinople were to send a missionary to preach Mohammedanism to us, he would find a pulpit at his service . . .

I happened soon after to attend one of his sermons, in the course of which I perceived he intended to finish with a collection, and I silently resolved he should get nothing from me. I had in my pocket a handful of copper money, three or four silver dollars, and five pistoles in gold. As he proceeded I began to soften, and concluded to give the coppers. Another stroke of his oratory made me ashamed of that, and determined me to give the silver; and he finished so admirably, that I emptied my pockets wholly into the collector's dish, gold and all. At this sermon there was also one of our club, who . . . suspecting a collection might be intended, had, by precaution, emptied his pockets before he came from home. Toward the conclusion of the discourse, however, he felt a strong desire to give, and applied to a neighbor, who stood near him, to borrow some money for the purpose. The application was unfortunately to perhaps the only man in the company who had the firmness not to be affected by the preacher. His answer was, "At any other time, Friend Hopkinson, I would lend to thee freely; but not now, for thee seems to be out of thy right senses."

He had a loud and clear voice, and articulated his words and sentences so perfectly, that he might be heard and understood at a great distance, especially as his auditors, however numerous, observed the most exact silence. He preached one evening from the top of the Courthouse steps . . . Both streets were filled with his hearers to a considerable distance . . . I had the curiousity to learn how far he could be heard, by retiring backward down the street towards the river; and I found his voice distinct till I came near Front Street, when some noise in the street obscured it . . . I computed that he might well be heard by more than thirty thousand. This reconciled me to newspaper accounts of his having preached to twenty-five thousand people in the fields . . .

140

His delivery . . . was so improved by frequent repetitions that every accent, every emphasis, every modulation of voice, was so perfectly well turned and well placed, that, without being interested in the subject, one could not help being pleased with the discourse; a pleasure of much the same kind with that received from an excellent piece of music.

GEORGE WHITEFIELD IN CONNECTICUT

A MIDDLETOWN FARMER

Now it pleased God to send Mr. Whitefield into this land and my hearing of his preaching at Philadelphia like one of the old apostles and many thousands flocking after him to hear the Gospel and great numbers were converted to Christ, I felt the spirit of God drawing me by conviction. I longed to see and hear him and wished he would come this way and I soon heard he was come to New York and the Jersies and great multitudes flocking after him under great concern for their souls and many converted which brought on my concern more and more, hoping soon to see him but next I heard he was on Long Island and next at Boston and next at Northampton, and then one morning all on a sudden about 8 or 9 o'clock, there came a messenger and said Mr. Whitefield preached at Hartford and Wethersfield yesterday and is to preach at Middletown this morning at 10 o'clock. I was in my field at work. I dropt my tool that I had in my hand and ran home and ran through my house and had my wife get ready quick to go and hear Mr. Whitefield preach at Middletown and ran to my pasture for my horse with all my might fearing I should be too late to hear him. I brought my horse home and soon mounted and took my wife up and went forward as fast as I thought the horse could bear and when my horse began to be out of breath I would get down and put my wife on the saddle and bid her ride as fast as she could and not stop or slack for me except I bade her and so I would run until I was almost out of breath and then mount my horse again and so I did several times to favor my horse. We improved every moment to get along as if we were fleeing for our lives, all this while fearing we should be too late to hear the sermon for we had twelve miles to ride double in little more than an hour and we went round by the upper parish and when we came within half a mile of the road that comes down from Hartford, Wethersfield, and Stepney to Middletown on high land I saw before me a cloud or fog rising, I first thought off from the Great River but as I came nearer the road I heard a noise something like a low rumbling thunder and I presently found it was the rumbling of horses feet coming down the road, and this cloud was a cloud of dust made by the running of horses feet, it arose some rods into the air over the tops of the hills and trees and when I came within about twenty rods of the road I could see men and horses slipping along in the cloud like shadows and when I came nearer it was like a steady stream of horses, and their riders, scarcely a horse more than his length behind another, all of a lather and foam with sweat, their breath rolling out of their nostrils, in a cloud of dust every jump, every horse seemed to go with all his might to carry his rider to hear the news from Heaven to the saving of their souls. It made me tremble to see the sight how the world was in a struggle. I found a vacance between two horses to slip in my horse and my wife said, "Law, our clothes will be all spoiled, see how they look"— for they was so covered with dust they looked almost all of a color, coats and hats and shirts and horses. We went down in the stream. I heard no man speak a word all the way, three miles, but every one pressing forward in great haste and when we got down to the old meeting-house there was a great multitude, it was said to be 3 or 4000 of people assembled together. We got off from our horses and shook off the dust and the ministers was then coming to the meeting-house. I turned and looked toward the Great River and saw the ferry boats running swift forward and backward bringing over loads of people, the oars rowed nimble and quick; everything, men, horses and boats seemed to be struggling for life; the land and the banks over the river looked black with people and horses. All along the twelve miles I see no man at work in his field but all seemed to be gone. When I see Mr. Whitefield come up upon the scaffold he looked almost angelical, a young slim slender youth before some thousands of people and with a bold undaunted countenance. And my hearing how God was with him everywhere as he came along it solemnized my mind and put me in a trembling fear before he began to preach for he looked as if he was clothed with authority from the great God and a sweet solemn Solemnity sat upon his brow, and my hearing him preach gave me a heart wound by God's blessing.

FROM THE JOURNAL OF
REV. FRANCIS ASBURY

Thursday, 10 [July 1788]. We had to cross the Allegheny mountain again, at a bad passage. Our course lay over mountains and through valleys, and the mud and mire was such as might scarcely be expected in December. We came to an old, forsaken habitation in Tyger's Valley. Here our horses grazed about, while we boiled our meat. Midnight brought us up at Jones's, after riding forty, or perhaps fifty miles. The old man, our host, was kind enough to wake us up at four o'clock in the morning. We journeyed on through devious lonely wilds, where no food might be found, except what grew in the woods, or was carried with us. We met with two women who were going to see their friends, and to attend the quarterly meeting at Clarksburg [West Virginia]. Near midnight we stopped at A——'s, who hissed his dogs at us: but the women were determined to get to quarterly meeting, so we went in. Our supper was tea. Brothers Phoebus and Cook took to the woods; old —— gave up his bed to the women. I lay along the floor on a few deerskins with the fleas. That night our poor horses got no corn; and next morning they had to swim across the Monongahela. After a twenty miles' ride we came to Clarksburg, and man and beast were so outdone that it took us ten hours to accomplish it. I lodged with Col. Jackson. Our meeting was held in a long, close room belonging to the Baptists. Our use of the house it seems gave offense. There attended about seven hundred people, to whom I preached with freedom; and I believe the Lord's power reached the hearts of some. After administering the sacrament, I was well satisfied to take my leave. We rode thirty miles to Father Haymond's, after three o'clock, Sunday afternoon, and made it nearly eleven before

145

we came in. About midnight we went to rest, and rose at five o'clock next morning. My mind has been severely tried under the great fatigue endured both by myself and my horse. O, how glad should I be of a plain, clean plank to lie on, as preferable to most of the beds; and where the beds are in a bad state, the floors are worse. The gnats are almost as troublesome here, as the mosquitoes in the lowlands of the seaboard. This country will require much work to make it tolerable. The people are, many of them, of the boldest cast of adventurers, and with some the decencies of civilized society are scarcely regarded, two instances of which I myself witnessed. The great landholders who are industrious will soon show the effects of the aristocracy of wealth, by lording it over their poorer neighbours, and by securing to themselves all the offices of profit or honour. On the one hand savage warfare teaches them to be cruel; and on the other, the preaching of Antinomians poisons them with error in doctrine: good moralists they are not, and good Christians they cannot be, unless they are better taught.

CIRCUIT RIDER

THOMAS WARE

During the mild season we had little inconvenience to encounter in travelling this circuit. But when the winter set in, our sufferings and privations were severe in the extreme. We had to cross Walker's mountain in our route. Early one morning, toward the close of the year, I commenced its steep ascent. Much rain had fallen the previous night; but it was a lovely morning, the air being exceedingly soft and pleasant for the season. When I gained the summit of a ridge or spur of the mountain, and looked toward the heights yet to be ascended, where winter was collecting its howling forces, my heart failed me, and I began to retrace my steps. Where I stood it was quite calm; and when I cast my eyes to the east, not a cloud was to be seen. But on the mountain's top all was raging tempest. The wind blew from the southwest, and the cloud, which had been hid from my view by the mountain, arose, and in thick and dark columns, loaded with vapour congealed into snow, which, as the sun shone upon it, had the appearance of a solid body of water, rolling in awful majesty, and threatening a general inundation. This, with the tremendous commotion of the agitated elements upon the summit of the mountain, presented the most terrific scene I had ever witnessed. I fled with all possible speed from this approaching cloud, which I supposed to be surcharged with rain; but it ultimately proved to be snow.

I then directed my course to the gap through which I had to pass; and being somewhat sheltered from the wind by the mountain, I supposed the storm had abated. But when I came to dispute this passage with the furious gale, pelting me with snow and hail at every step, it called for all the resolution I possessed to force the defile in the face of so formidable a foe. It was almost night when I came in sight of the hamlet for which I had long been anxiously looking; but, alas! a creek which crossed the way had so swollen by the late rain that I could not pass it. The sun had gone down clear; and the cold was intense, and becoming more so every minute. I called aloud for assistance until I became hoarse; but no one answered. Seeing near me a few stacks of hay, with a number of cattle shivering around them, as they appeared to be my only resort to save myself from perishing, and furnish my horse with something to eat, I repaired to them, placed my horse in a situation to eat, and provided as well as I could to make myself a bed of the hay to spend the night, unless some one should come to feed the stock, who might assist me over the creek. It was soon dark, and no one came. My blood began to be chilled; and I felt that to stay there was to jeopard my life. So I resolved on returning to a sorry-looking hut which I had seen about five miles back, and seek for shelter there. I found the hut warm, and inhabited·by a young couple with two small children. Whether they thought me intoxicated, or what else, (as the cold had very much affected my speech,) I do not know; but the man gave me to understand, at once, that I could not stay there. I looked at him, and smiling, said, that would depend upon our comparative strength. It was true he might demand the assistance of his wife to put me out; but I fondly hoped she would be on my side. At this he laughed pleasantly, and began to stir up the fire. When they ascertained who I was they treated me with great kindness, and furnished me every thing in their power to render me and my beast comfortable. In the morning I baptized their children; and the man kindly accompanied me to a safe fording place, where I crossed, and soon reached the house of a friend, where I had an appointment the preceding day. But my sufferings ended not with that day, nor have they terminated yet. My feet were sore for a long time; and they have ever since been subject to a deathlike coldness, for which there is no remedy this side of the grave.

DEACON BALLARD'S MILL

JULIA SHELLEY HODGES

His mill was a consecrated place. His Bible had a niche there, and his Village Hymn Book, yellowed and thumbed all over, was his constant companion. Many a man who brought his sack of wool to be carded, carried something better than it away—a word of encouragement or exhortation, of warning, as circumstances required. It is true of him that many names of impenitent men, written out on slips of paper, were carried about, from day to day, if not from year to year, in his pocket, and made the subject of earnest prayer. Some of these were converted, and others, as it would seem, had all the harder work to resist the strivings of the Holy Spirit, for his prayers. So well known was this fact, that Christians and sometimes the unbelievers were heard to say: "there is hope for this and that hardened sinner, for their names are in Deacon Ballard's pocket." Not a man of learning, but, someone said, "a man with one talent—his knowledge of the Bible."

LETTER FROM KENTUCKY (1802)

G. A. BAXTER

On my way to Kentucky, I was told by settlers on the road, that the character of Kentucky travellers was entirely changed, and that they were now as distinguished for sobriety as they had formerly been for dissoluteness; and indeed, I found Kentucky the most moral place I had ever been in; a profane expression was hardly heard; a religious awe seemed to pervade the country; and some deistical characters had confessed that from whatever cause the revival might originate, it certainly made the people better. Its influence was not less visible in promoting a friendly temper; nothing could appear more amiable than that undissembled benevolence which governs the subjects of this work. I have often wished that the mere politician or deist could observe with impartiality their peaceful and amicable spirit. He would certainly see that nothing could equal the religion of Jesus for promoting even the temporal happiness of society. Some neighborhoods visited by the revival had been formerly notorious for private animosities, and many petty lawsuits had commenced on that ground. When the parties in those quarrels were impressed with religion, the first thing was to send for their antagonists; and it was often very affecting to see their meeting. Both had seen their faults, and both contended that they ought to make concessions, till at last they were obliged to request each to forbear all mention of the past, and to act as friends and brothers for the future. Now, sir, let modern philosophists talk of reforming the world by banishing Christianity and introducing

150

their licentious systems. The blessed gospel of our God and Saviour is showing what it can do.

Some circumstances have concurred to distinguish the Kentucky revival from most others of which we have any account. I mean the largeness of the assemblies on sacramental occasions, the length of time they continued on the ground in devotional exercises, and the great numbers who have fallen down under religious impressions. On each of these particulars I shall make some remarks.

1st. With respect to the largeness of the assemblies. It is generally supposed that at many places there were not fewer than eight, ten, or twelve thousand people. At a place called Cane Ridge Meeting-House, many are of opinion there were at least twenty thousand. There were 140 wagons which came loaded with people, besides other wheel carriages. Some persons had come 200 miles. The largeness of these assemblies was an inconvenience—they were too numerous to be addressed by one speaker; it therefore became necessary for several ministers to officiate at the same time at different stands. This afforded an opportunity to those who were but slightly impressed with religion to wander to and fro between the different places of worship, which created an appearance of confusion, and gave ground to such as were unfriendly to the work to charge it with disorder.

Another cause also conduced to the same effect; about this time, the people began to fall down in great numbers, under serious impressions. This was a new thing among Presbyterians; it excited universal astonishment, and created a curiosity which could not be restrained, when people fell even during the most solemn parts of divine service. Those who stood near, were so extremely anxious to see how they were affected, that they often crowded about them, so as to disturb the worship. But these causes of disorder were soon removed; different sacraments were appointed on the same Sabbath, which divided the people, and falling down became so familiar as to excite no disturbance. In October, I attended three sacraments; at each, there were supposed to be four or five thousand people, and everything was conducted with strict propriety. When persons fell, those who were near took care of them, and everything continued quiet until the worship was concluded.

2d. The length of time that people continue at the places of worship, is another important circumstance of the Kentucky revival. At Cane Ridge they met on Friday, and continued till Wednesday evening, night and day, without intermission, either in public or private exercises of devotion, and with such earnestness, that heavy showers of rain were not sufficient to disperse them. On other sacramental occasions, they generally continued on the ground until Monday or Tuesday evening; and had not the preachers been exhausted and obliged to retire, or had they chosen to prolong the worship, they might have kept the people any length of time they pleased; and all this was or might have been done in a country where, less than twelve months before, the clergy found it difficult to detain the people during the usual exercises of the Sabbath.

The practice of camping on the ground was introduced partly by necessity, and partly by inclination; the assemblies were generally too large to be received by any common neighborhood; everything indeed was done which hospitality and brotherly kindness could do, to accommodate the people; public and private houses were opened, and free invitations given to all persons who wished to retire. Farmers gave up their meadows, before they were mown, to supply the horses; yet, notwithstanding all this liberality, it would have been impossible, in many cases, to have accommodated the whole assemblies with private lodgings; but, besides, the people were unwilling to suffer any interruption in their devotions, and they formed an attachment to the place where they were continually seeing so many careless sinners receiving their first impressions, and so many deists constrained to call on the formerly despised name of Jesus; they conceived a a sentiment like what Jacob felt in Bethel, "Surely the Lord is in this place." "This is none other but the house of God, and this is the gate of heaven."

3rd. The number of persons who have fallen down under

152

serious impressions in this revival, is another matter worthy of attention; and on this I shall be more particular, as it seems to be the principal cause why this work should be more suspected of enthusiasm than some other revivals. At Cane Ridge sacrament, it is generally supposed not less than one thousand persons fell prostrate to the ground, among whom were many infidels. At one sacrament which I attended, the number that fell was thought to be more than three hundred. Persons who fall, are generally such as had manifested symptoms of the deepest impressions for some time previous to that event. It is common to see them shed tears plentifully for about an hour. Immediately before they become totally powerless, they are seized with a tremor, and sometimes, though not often, they utter one or two piercing shrieks, in the moment of falling; persons in this situation are affected in different degrees; sometimes, when unable to stand or sit, they have the use of their hands, and can converse with perfect composure. In other cases they are unable to speak, the pulse becomes weak, and they draw a difficult breath, about once in a minute: in some instances, their extremities become cold, and pulsation, breathing, and all the signs of life forsake them for nearly an hour. Persons who have been in this situation have uniformly avowed that they felt no bodily pain, that they had the entire use of their reason and reflection, and when recovered, they could relate everything that had been said or done near them, or which could possibly fall within their observation.

From this it appears that their falling is neither common fainting, nor a nervous action. Indeed this strange phenomenon appears to have taken every possible turn to baffle the conjectures of those who are not willing to consider it a supernatural work. Persons have sometimes fallen on their way from public worship; and sometimes after they had arrived home; and in some cases when they were pursuing their common business on their farms, or when they retired for secret devotion. It was observed that persons generally are seriously affected for some time previous to their falling; in many cases, however, it is otherwise. Numbers of thoughtless sinners have fallen as suddenly as if struck with lightning. Many professed infidels, and other vicious characters have been arrested in this way, and sometimes at the very time they were uttering blasphemies against the work.

At the beginning of the revival in Shelby County, the appearances, as related to me by eye-witness, were very surprising indeed. The revival had before this spread with irresistible power through the adjacent counties; and many of the pious had attended distant sacraments with great benefit. These were much engaged, and felt unusual freedom in their addresses at the throne of grace, for the out-pouring of the divine Spirit at the approaching sacrament in Shelby. The sacrament came on in September. The people as usual met on Friday: but all were languid, and the exercises went on heavily. On Saturday and Sunday morning it was no better. At length the communion service commenced, everything was still lifeless: whilst the minister of the place was speaking at one of the tables, without any unusual animation, suddenly there were several shrieks from different parts of the assembly; instantly persons fell in every direction; the feelings of the pious were suddenly revived, and the work progressed with extraordinary power, till the conclusion of the solemnity. This phenomenon of falling is common to all ages, sexes, and characters; and when they fall they are differently exercised. Some pious people have fallen under a sense of ingratitude and hardness of heart, and others under affecting manifestations of the love and goodness of God. Many thoughtless persons under legal convictions, have obtained comfort before they arose.

But perhaps the most numerous class consists of those who fall under distressing views of their guilt, who arise with the same fearful apprehensions, and continue in that state for some days, perhaps weeks, before they receive comfort. I have conversed with many who fell under the influence of comfortable feelings, and the account they gave of their exercises while they lay entranced was very surprising. I know not how to give you a better idea of them than by saying, that in many cases they appeared to surpass the dying exercises of Dr. Finley; their minds appeared wholly swallowed up in contemplating the perfections of Deity, as illustrated in the plan of salvation, and whilst they lay apparently senseless, and almost lifeless, their minds were more vigorous, and their memories more retentive and accurate than they had ever been before.

I have heard men of respectability assert that their manifestations of gospel truth were so clear, as to require some caution when they began to speak, lest they should use language which might induce their hearers to suppose, that they had seen those things with their bodily eyes; but at the same time they had seen no image, nor sensible representation, nor indeed any thing besides the old truths contained in the Bible. Among those whose minds were filled with the most delightful communications of divine love, I but seldom observed anything ecstatic. Their expressions were just and rational, they conversed with calmness and composure, and on their first recovering the use of speech, they appeared like persons recovering from a violent disease which had left them on the borders of the grave. I have sometimes been present when persons who fell under the influence of convictions, obtained relief before they arose; in these cases it was impossible not to observe how strongly the change in their minds was depicted in their countenances. Instead of a face of horror and despair, they assumed one open, luminous, serene and expressive of all the comfortable feelings of religion. As to those who fall down under legal convictions and continue in that state, they are not different from those who receive convictions in other revivals, excepting that their distress is more severe. Indeed extraordinary power is the leading characteristic of this revival; both saints and sinners have more striking discoveries of the realities of another world, than I have ever known on any other occasion.

PIGEON CHURCH

CARL SANDBURG

A mile across the fields from the Lincoln home was the Pigeon church, a log-built meeting-house put up in 1822. . . . To the members, the Bible, and the lands, names, stories, texts, and teachings of the Bible, were overshadowing realities, to be read, thought over, interpreted, and used in daily life. To "grow in grace" and to arrive at "grace abounding," to be "strong in sperrit," to "cast out delusion," were matters connected definitely with the daily life of arising, building a fire, breaking the ice sheets on water, and starting a kettle to boil, and then going forth to the chores of the barn and the horse-trough, the corn-crib, the pigpen. Such biblical words as "malice," "mercy," and "charity" were topics of long explanations.

Most of the church people could read only the shortest words in the Bible, or none at all. They sat in the log meeting-house on the split-log benches their own axes had shaped, listening to the preacher reading from the Bible by the light of fire-logs. The pronunciation of the words Egypt, Mesopotamia, Babylon, Damascus, set minds to work imagining places less real to them than Rockport, Boonville, Vincennes, Cincinnati. Epithets and texts enunciated often by preachers became tissues of their spiritual lives; the words meant something beyond the actual words in "weeping and wailing and gnashing of teeth," "an eye for an eye, and a tooth for a tooth," "by the waters of Babylon." They could see the direct inference to be drawn from, "The fathers have eaten sour grapes and the children's teeth are set on edge," or the suggestions in "Let not your heart be troubled," or "Let him who is without sin cast the first stone," or "As you would that others should do unto you, do ye even so unto them."

Their own morning-glories, honeysuckle, and blooming perennials came to leafage out of the rhythmic text, "Consider the lilies of the field, how they grow; they toil not, neither do they spin; and yet I say unto you, that even Solomon in all his glory was not arrayed like one of these." They felt enough portents in the two words, "Jesus wept," for the arrangement of that as a verse by itself.

At the Pigeon church one of the favorite hymns was "How Tedious and Tasteless the Hours," and another, "Oh, to Grace How Great a Debtor!" and another began with the lines:

> When I can read my title clear
> To mansions in the skies.

To confess, to work hard, to be saving, to be decent, were the actions most praised and pleaded for in the sermons of the preachers. Next to denying Christ, the worst sins were drinking, gambling, fighting, loafing, among the men, and gossiping, backbiting, sloth, and slack habits among the women. A place named Hell where men, women, and children burned everlastingly in fires was the place where sinners would go.

In a timber grove one summer Sunday afternoon, a preacher yelled, shrieked, wrung his hands in sobs of hysterics, until a row of women were laid out to rest and recover in the shade of an oak-tree, after they had moaned, shaken, danced up and down, worn themselves out with "the jerks" and fainted. And young Abe Lincoln, looking on, with sober face and quiet heart, was thoughtful about what he saw before his eyes.

The Sabbath was not only a day for religious meetings. After the sermon, the members, who rode horses many miles to the meeting-house, talked about crops, weather, births and deaths, the growing settlements, letters just come, politics, Indians, and land-titles.

Families had prayers in the morning on arising, grace at breakfast, noon prayers and grace at dinner, grace at supper, and evening prayers at bedtime. In those households, the manger at Bethlehem was a white miracle, the Black Friday at Golgotha and the rocks rolled away for the Resurrection were near-by realities

157

of terror and comfort, dark power and sustenance. The Sabbath day, Christmas, Easter, were days for sober thoughts and sober faces, resignation, contemplation, rest, silence. Verses in the Gospel of St. John had rhythm and portent. "I am the way, the truth, and the life. . . . He that believeth in me shall not perish but shall have everlasting life."

Besides a wisdom of short syllables covering all the wants of life in the Lord's Prayer, they found a melodious movement of musical intention in the arrangement of its simple words. It was like a walk from a green valley to a great mountain to pronounce with thoughtful cadence: "Give us this day our daily bread. And forgive us our trespasses as we forgive those who trespass against us. And lead us not into temptation but deliver us from evil."

The glisten of dewdrops on wheat straws, in the gray chill of daybreak on harvest fields, shone in the solemn assurance of, "Yea, though I walk through the valley of the shadow of death, I will fear no evil: . . . they rod and thy staff they comfort me."

There was occupation of the imaginative gift, a challenge even to the sleeping or crying senses of color and form, hidden in the picture of Jacob's ladder stretching from the man in earth-slumber up beyond the limits of sky; in the drama of Jonah entering the belly of the whale and later issuing forth from that darkness; in the swift stride of the four horsemen of the apocalypse; in the coat of many colors worn by Joseph and the dream of seven years of famine to come upon Egypt; in the flawless and clear-eyed sheep-boy David, walking with sling and stone to win battle against the stiff-necked giant Goliath by reason of one fierce stone pounded home to the forehead of the swaggerer; in the massive prefigurements of preparation for calamity or destruction of mortal pride to be found in the episodes of Noah's ark and the upthrust and come-down of the Tower of Babel.

After a day of plowing corn, picking potato bugs, whittling beanpoles, capturing strayed cattle and fixing up a hole in a snake-rail fence, while the housewife made a kettle of soap, hoed the radishes and cabbages, milked the cows, and washed the baby, there was a consolation leading to easy slumber in the beatitudes: "Blessed are the meek: for they shall inherit the earth. . . . Blessed are the pure in heart, for they shall see God. Blessed are the peacemakers: for they shall be called the children of God." It was not their business to be sure of the arguments and the invincible logic that might underlie the Bible promises of heaven and threats of hell; it was for this the preacher was hired and paid by the corn, wheat, whisky, pork, linen, wool, and other produce brought by the members of the church.

The exquisite foretokening, "In my Father's house are many mansions: if it were not so I would have told you," was but a carrying farther of the implications of that cry from the ramparts of the unconquerable, "O death, where is thy sting? O grave, where is thy victory?"

Beyond Indiana was something else; beyond the timber and underbrush, the malaria, milk-sick, blood, sweat, tears, hands hard and crooked as the roots of walnut trees, there must be something else.

THE BIBLE AND ABRAHAM LINCOLN

CARL SANDBURG

When death was close by, and there was a murmur out of deep rivers, and the moan of a long wind out of a cavern of dark stars, Lincoln often used Bible language.

The young printer, Gilbert J. Greene, drove out with him from Springfield one time to a farmhouse where a woman was dying. Lincoln was to draw up her last will and testament. After the paper was signed and witnessed, as the young printer remembered what happened, the woman asked, "Mr. Lincoln, won't you read a few verses out of the Bible for me?"

A Bible was brought; but, instead of taking it, the lawyer began reciting from memory the psalm, "Though I walk through the valley of the shadow of death I will fear no evil, for thou art with me; thy rod and thy staff they comfort me." And again, without taking the Bible, he repeated such verses as, "Let not your heart be troubled; ye believe in God, believe also in me," and "In my Father's house are many mansions; if it were not so I would have told you. I go to prepare a place for you."

He had told Mrs. Rankin, over near New Salem, that before he learned to read as a boy he had heard his mother saying over certain Bible verses day by day as she worked. He had learned these verses by heart; the tones of his mother's voice were in them; and sometimes, as he read these verses, he seemed to hear the voice of Nancy Hanks speaking them. This he told Mrs. Rankin one day when a Sunday-school convention was being held at Petersburg and the question was discussed as to the age at which children were morally responsible and prepared to be taught the Bible.

THE BATTLE HYMN OF THE REPUBLIC

JULIA WARD HOWE

Mine eyes have seen the glory of the coming of the Lord:
He is trampling out the vintage where the grapes of wrath are
    stored;
He has loosed the fateful lightning of his terrible swift sword.
    His truth is marching on.

I have seen him in the watch-fires of a hundred circling camps;
They have builded him an altar in the evening dews and damps;
I can read his righteous sentence by the dim and flaring lamps.
    His day is marching on.

I have read a fiery gospel, writ in burnished rows of steel:
"As ye deal with my contemners, so with you my grace shall deal;
Let the Hero, born of woman, crush the serpent with his heel,
    Since God is marching on."

He has sounded forth the trumpet that shall never call retreat;
He is sifting out the hearts of men before his judgment seat:
O, be swift, my soul to answer him! be jubilant my feet!
    Our God is marching on.

In the beauty of the lilies Christ was born across the sea,
With a glory in his bosom that transfigures you and me;
As he died to make men holy, let us die to make men free,
    While God is marching on.

THE RELIGION OF ROBERT E. LEE

DOUGLAS SOUTHALL FREEMAN

Kindness was the first implication of religion in his mind—not the deliberate kindness of "good works" to pacify exacting Deity, but the instinctive kindness of a heart that had been schooled to regard others. His was not a nature to waste time in the perplexities of self-analysis; but if those about him at headquarters had understood him better they might often have asked themselves whether, when he brought a refreshing drink to a dusty lieutenant who called with dispatches, he was discharging the social duty of a host or was giving a "cup of cold water" in his Master's name. His manner in either case would have been precisely the same.

Equally was his religion expressed in his unquestioning response to duty. In his clear creed, right was duty and must be discharged. "There is," he wrote down privately for his own guidance, "a true glory and a true honor: the glory of duty done—the honor of the integrity of principle." He probably never summed up this aspect of his religion more completely than in that self-revealing hour before he started to meet General Grant, when he answered all the appeals of his lieutenants with the simple statement: "The question is, is it right to surrender this army? If it is right, then I will take all the responsibility." It was a high creed—right at all times and at all costs—but daily self-discipline and a clear sense of justice made him able to adhere to it.

Humility was another major implication of his religion. So lofty was his conception of man's duty to his Maker and to his neighbors, so completely did his ambition extend, all unconsciously, into the realm of the spirit, that he was never satisfied with what he was. Those who stood with him on the red field of Appomattox thought that his composure was due to his belief that he had discharged his full duty, and in this they were partially correct; but he always felt, with a sincerity no man can challenge, that he had fallen immeasurably short of his ideal of a servant of God. "So humble was he as a Christian," wrote Mrs. Lee on the day of his death, "that he said not long ago to me he wished he felt sure of his acceptance. I said all who love and trust in the Savior need not fear. He did not reply, but a more upright and conscientious Christian never lived."

KEEPING THE SABBATH

HENRY WARD BEECHER

The saw was ripping away yesterday in the carpenter's shop and the hammer was noisy enough. Today there is not a sign of life there. The anvil makes no music today. The mill is silent. Only the brook continues noisy. And the birds are all singing— larks, robins, blackbirds, orioles, sparrows, and bluebirds; mocking catbirds and wrens, singing as on no other day but Sunday when other sounds are still.

There was no sound in the village store. Look either way—not a wagon; not a human being. The smoke rose up soberly and quietly as if it said, "It's Sunday." The leaves on the great elms, hung motionless, glittering in the dew, as if they too were waiting for the bell to ring for meeting, and when the first bell rang, the sound rolled over and over through the air, twice as far as on week days. There were no less than seven steeples in sight from the belfry, and the sexton said when the wind was right he had heard all seven.

At meeting time the empty streets suddenly were filled but there was no fevered hurry. All blossomed in their best like a rosebud in June. Do you know that man in the silk hat and new black coat? Probably it is some stranger. No, it is the carpenter who was racing about yesterday with his sleeves rolled up and a dust and business look in his face. And there's the blacksmith— does he not look every inch a judge now that he is clean washed, shaved and dressed? His eyes are as bright as the sparks that fly from his anvil.

SUNDAY DRESS

JANE ADDAMS

Although I constantly confided my sins and perplexities to my father, there are only a few occasions on which I remember having received direct advice or admonition; it may easily be true, however, that I have forgotten the latter, in the manner of many seekers after advice who enjoyably set forth their situation but do not really listen to the advice itself. I can remember an admonition on one occasion, however, when, as a little girl of eight years, arrayed in a new cloak, gorgeous beyond anything I had ever worn before, I stood before my father for his approval. I was much chagrined by his remark that it was a very pretty cloak—in fact so much prettier than any cloak the other little girls in the Sunday School had, that he would advise me to wear my old cloak, which would keep me quite as warm, with the added advantage of not making the other little girls feel badly. I complied with the request but I fear without inner consent, and I certainly was quite without the joy of self-sacrifice as I walked soberly through the village street by the side of my counselor. My mind was busy, however, with the old question eternally suggested by the inequalities of the human lot. Only as we neared the church door did I venture to ask what could be done about it, receiving the reply that it might never be righted so far as clothes went, but that people might be equal in things that mattered much more than clothes, the affairs of education and religion, for instance, which we attended to when we went to school and church, and that it was very stupid to wear the sort of clothes that made it harder to have equality even there.

GENERAL WILLIAM BOOTH
ENTERS INTO HEAVEN

VACHEL LINDSAY

(*To be sung to the tune of "The Blood of the Lamb" with indicated instrument*)

I

(*Bass drum beaten loudly.*)
Booth led boldly with his big bass drum—
(Are you washed in the blood of the Lamb?)
The Saints smiled gravely and they said: "He's come."
(Are you washed in the blood of the Lamb?)
Walking lepers followed, rank on rank,
Lurching bravos from the ditches dank,
Drabs from the alleyways and drug fiends pale—
Minds still passion-ridden, soul-powers frail:—
Vermin-eaten saints with mouldy breath,
Unwashed legions with the ways of Death—
(Are you washed in the blood of the Lamb?)

(*Banjos.*)
Every slum had sent its half-a-score
The round world over. (Booth had groaned for more.)
Every banner that the wide world flies
Bloomed with glory and transcendent dyes.
Big-voiced lasses made their banjos bang,
Tranced, fanatical they shrieked and sang:—
"Are you washed in the blood of the Lamb?"

Hallelujah! It was queer to see
Bull-necked convicts with that land make free.
Loons with trumpets blowed a blare, blare, blare
On, on upward thro' the golden air!
(Are you washed in the blood of the Lamb?)

II

(Bass drum slower and softer.)
Booth died blind and still by faith he trod,
Eyes still dazzled by the ways of God.
Booth led boldly, and he looked the chief
Eagle countenance in sharp relief,
Beard a-flying, air of high command
Unabated in that holy land.

(Sweet flute music.)
Jesus came from out the court-house door,
Stretched his hands above the passing poor.
Booth saw not, but led his queer ones there
Round and round the mighty court-house square.
Then, in an instant all that blear review
Marched on spotless, clad in raiment new.
The lame were straightened, withered limbs uncurled
And blind eyes opened on a new, sweet world.

(Bass drum louder.)
Drabs and vixens in a flash made whole!
Gone was the weasel-head, the snout, the jowl!
Sages and sibyls now, and athletes clean,
Rulers of empires, and of forests green!

*(Grand chorus of all instruments. Tambourines to the fore-
ground.)*
The hosts were sandalled, and their wings were fire!
(Are you washed in the blood of the Lamb?)
But their noise played havoc with the angel-choir.

(Are you washed in the blood of the Lamb?)
Oh, shout Salvation! It was good to see
Kings and Princes by the Lamb set free.
The banjos rattled and the tambourines
Jing-jing-jingled in the hands of Queens.

(*Reverently sung, no instruments.*)
And when Booth halted by the curb for prayer
He saw his master thro' the flag-filled air.
Christ came gently with a robe and crown
For Booth the soldier, while the throng knelt down.
He saw King Jesus. They were face to face,
And he knelt a-weeping in that holy place.
Are you washed in the blood of the Lamb?

THE NEW EVANGELIST

TIME, THE WEEKLY NEWSMAGAZINE

The first one to come forward was a round, sensible-looking housewife with thick glasses. She stood as still and undramatic as if she were waiting to be served at the meat counter. The next was an eleven-year-old boy who kept his head low to hide his tears; a thin girl appeared behind him and put her hand comfortingly on his shoulder. These three were joined by a broad-shouldered young man whose machine-knitted jersey celebrated a leaping swordfish, then by a pretty young Negro woman in her best clothes with a sleeping baby in her arms. Suddenly there were too many to count, standing on the trampled grass in the blaze of lights. Some of them wept quietly, some of them stared at the ground and some looked upward.

Above them all stood a tall, blond young man in a double-breasted tan gabardine suit. His handsome, strong-jawed face was drawn and his blue eyes glittered; for a few seconds he gnawed nervously on a thumbnail, and bright sweat covered his high forehead. He was speaking softly, but with an urgency that seemed to tense every muscle of his body:

"You can leave here with peace and joy and happiness such as you've never known. You say: 'Well, Billy, that's all well and good. I'll think it over and I may come back some night and I'll—' Wait a minute! You can't come to Christ any time you want to. You can only come when the Spirit of God is drawing and wooing you . . . I beg of you to come now before it is too late. You know you need Christ in your life. Leave your seat now and come forward. If you have friends or relatives here, they'll wait on you. Whether you're old or young, or rich or poor, white or colored—come quietly up now and say, 'Billy, tonight I accept Christ.' "

From Savonarola to Billy Sunday, evangelists have exhorted sinners to repentance and preached salvation as a right-now, yes-or-no decision. The hot Gospel played a major part in the making of America, when churches were fewer, distances vast and life hard. But upper-crust Christians tend to regard the sweaty urgency of evangelistic Christianity as frequently hypocritical and always in bad taste. Billy Graham is different.

He preaches with his shirt collar unbuttoned, so that "my Adam's apple can move up and down." Yet he always looks immaculately pressed and groomed. He is surrounded by electronics—a tiny portable microphone to pick up his voice while he preaches (with a wire clipped to his belt loop), batteries of dictaphones for dictation, the whole Bible on records. And yet he never sounds mechanical and often seems old-fashioned. He unblushingly applies the hard-sell technique to God ("I'm selling," he says, "the greatest product in the world; why shouldn't it be promoted as well as soap?"). And yet such eminently low-pressure, dignity-bound clerics as the Archbishop of Canterbury have given Graham their blessing. A farewell dinner given for him in London . . . included 70 peers and peeresses, and even the austerely intellectual *Manchester Guardian* admitted, "He has a holy simplicity."

How does he do it? Billy would be able to answer that one right off, and with deep sincerity: by the grace of God. "If God should take His hands off my life," says Billy, "my lips would turn to clay. I'm no great intellectual, and there are thousands of men who are better preachers than I am. You can't explain me if you leave out the supernatural. I am but a tool of God."

The religion most prevalent in our northern colonies is a refinement on the principles of resistance: it is the dissidence of dissent, and the protestantism of the Protestant religion.

Edmund Burke (1729–97)

The Meaning of Protestantism

When Edmund Burke made his famous speech in the British Parliament on conciliation with the American colonies, he emphasized how much Protestant traditions enter into the thinking of all Americans.

In those days, of course, almost all the colonists were Protestants. Although America was already a haven for religious refugees, there were only some 25,000 Roman Catholics and 2,000 Jews in the colonies at the time of the Revolution. Today, one out of every four church members belongs to the Roman Catholic Church and one out of every 30 is Jewish. Yet the Protestant tradition affects their lives and thinking as it does that of other Americans.

What, then, is Protestantism? That which follows represents some of the possible answers.

171

WHAT IS PROTESTANTISM?

ROBERT MCAFEE BROWN

The verb "to protest" comes from the Latin *protestari*, and means not only "to testify," but, more importantly, "to testify *on behalf of* something." *Webster's Dictionary* gives as a synonym, "to affirm." The *Oxford English Dictionary* defines it, "to declare formally in public, testify, to make a solemn declaration." The notion of a "protest against error" is only a subsidiary meaning. Thus the actual word itself is charged with positive rather than negative connotations. "To protest," then, in the true meaning of the word, is to make certain affirmations, to give testimony on behalf of certain things. . . . The image of Protestantism as protest against fails to do justice to the intent of the Protestant Reformers. If the reformers were *against* certain things, it was only because they were primarily *for* certain other things. The very term "Protestant" was first used at the Imperial Diet of Speyer (1529) by a minority group of Lutherans who disagreed with the majority decision to curtail their rights, and who therefore "protested." But if we read their statement carefully, we discover that they were making rousingly positive assertions. If they rejected churchmanship under the papacy, it was only because they believed that true churchmanship must be exercised under Scripture:

There is, we affirm, no sure preaching or doctrine but that which abides by the Word of God. According to God's command no other doctrine should be preached. Each text of the holy and divine scriptures should be elucidated and

172

explained by other texts. This Holy Book is in all things necessary for the Christian; it shines clearly in its own light, and is found to enlighten the darkness. We are determined by God's grace and aid to abide by God's Word alone, the Holy Gospel contained in the Biblical books of the Old and New Testaments. This Word alone should be preached, and nothing that is contrary to it. It is the only Truth. It is the sure rule of all Christian doctrine and conduct. It can never fail us or deceive us. Whoso builds and abides on this foundation shall stand against all the gates of hell, while all merely human additions and vanities set up against it must fall before the presence of God.

There can be a venturesomeness in Protestant life and thought that often seems to the non-Protestant Christian to get out of bounds. But it is in this area that new advances, new insights, new understandings of the faith grow. Very often the man who first appears as a heretic turns out to be the one who was recalling Christendom to a long-neglected truth. He may have shouted a little too loudly, as the only way of getting a hearing, but had he not shouted, had he not rocked the boat a little, his fellow Christians might not have become aware that they were heading for dangerous shoals. Protestantism has an obligation to suffer fools gladly lest it stifle the message of one who is a "fool for Christ."

Protestants do not say, "We have arrived," they say, "We are on the way." The Christian life, as Protestants know it, does not have a last chapter. It is a constant succession of new chapters. Its theme is not an arrival, but a series of departures. It is the story of a pilgrimage.

The spirit of Protestantism [is] an openness to the judging and renewing activity of the living God made known in Jesus Christ. Protestantism at its best is willing to submit to the corrective activity of God, and to hold all things of no account so long as he is honored, which also means to hold all things in honor that can be used by him. The spirit of Protestantism involves a willingness to live at risk, not only because the claim to human security is a denial of God, but because when human securities have been destroyed, God can enter in.

A DEFINITION

H. M. GWATKIN

Protestantism. I. Derivation and definition. The Lat. *protestari*, a post-Augustan word found in Quintilian and frequently in law, means 'to profess,' 'bear witness (or declare) openly,' so that it is nearly equivalent to *profiteri;* in both cases the preposition adds the idea of openness or publicity to that of witness or declaration. It has no inherent negative force as a protest against something, though it is often used in law as though the speaker's meaning has been misunderstood.

FROM PRIMER FOR PROTESTANTS

JAMES HASTINGS NICHOLS

Protestantism also represents a genuine revival of the life and gospels of the apostles, and even a continuation of certain major streams of religious life of the Latin middle ages. On several important issues Protestantism is in the main line of Western Christian history and it is modern Romanism which represents the innovation and "protest." Modern Roman Catholicism was radically reorganized in creed, government, and worship in reaction to the Reformation, and is historically incomprehensible save as a protest against Protestantism. Many peripheral aspects of the life of the undivided church which the Reformation had attacked or belittled were now deliberately moved into the center of emphasis and many novelties established. A new denomination was created, as "Protestant" in the negative sense as Lutheranism or Calvinism, and yet like them having also certain roots and precedents in the undivided church. Modern Romanism and modern Protestantism alike are partly revolutionary and partly traditional and neither can be fully understood without relating it to the other.

As André Siegfried wrote, Protestantism is America's "only national religion, and to ignore that fact is to view the country from a false angle."

The true apostolic succession lies not in external and official devolution from the apostles, but in being like them.

THE GENIUS OF PROTESTANTISM

SAMUEL MCCREA CAVERT

The genius of the Protestant movement . . . is positive and creative. The Reformation was not merely an episode in history; it initiated a process that is still going on. It should be regarded less as a consummation than as a beginning. By its fresh recovery of vital aspects of the Christian gospel, it released a new spirit that has been and still is a powerful ferment not only in the Church but also in society at large. The central insights of the Reformation are a continuing part both of dynamic Christianity and of the cultural heritage of the Western world.

To interpret this common heritage is a part of the function of the chapters that follow. It is in order here, however, to suggest briefly some of the basic insights that give inner unity and coherence to Protestantism as a whole:

1. Protestantism, in all its historic forms, insists upon the immediacy of man's relation with God. That relation rests on the unmerited grace of God, revealed to men in Jesus Christ and appropriated by them through faith in him. Man's reconciliation with God is something man does not initiate but joyously accepts as the freely offered gift of God.

2. Protestantism, in its many diverse expressions, holds that the Scriptures provide the decisive norm of spiritual authority. Read with the eye of faith and illumined by the guidance of the Holy Spirit, they offer to the individual Christian a saving knowledge of God and his will for human life.

3. All Protestants agree that there is a universal priesthood of believers. Since every Christian may receive in faith the gift of

177

God's redeeming love in Christ, as recorded in the Scriptures, he is not dependent on priest or ecclesiastical rites but may exercise the right and duty of private judgment. This means a high emphasis upon the principle of individuality.

4. All Protestants stress the importance of religious freedom. They resist coercion, whether by political or ecclesiastical power, in matters of religious faith and practice. This makes Protestantism especially congenial to democracy. Both require the free assent of the individual.

Two further points, less widely recognized, call for special attention:

1. Protestantism tends to place a new valuation upon common life and labor. It recognizes no basic separation between the "religious" and the "secular" vocation. It regards all men as equally called to serve God in their daily occupations. It thus stresses the principle of Christian stewardship in all earthly callings.

2. Protestantism believes in the Church. The charge is often made that Protestantism so overemphasizes the individual as to produce an atomistic result, with no real doctrine of the Church. It must be acknowledged that this is the point at which Protestants have been weakest. The full synthesis of liberty and unity has never been achieved by either Catholicism or Protestantism. But the ecumenical movement of today is a clear indication that Protestantism cherishes the ideal of *community* as well as of *individuality*. If the note of the universal fellowship of all the people of Christ is late in coming to adequate embodiment, we can at least rejoice that it has now clearly emerged into the Protestant consciousness. Protestantism always leaves room for free criticism of the Church in the light of God's revelation of his will in Christ but at the same time struggles for the realization of the Christian community as one Body of Christ throughout the world.

THE PROTESTANT SPIRIT

DONALD G. MILLER

Protestantism is not an event but a spirit; not the appearance of a new phenomenon at any particular stage of history, but the outcropping again and again, in successive stages of history, of the unquenchable yearning of the human spirit for vital fellowship with God. Essential Protestantism was not born when a heroic young monk dramatically nailed to the door of the Wittenberg Cathedral a list of ninety-five challenges to medievalism. That was a renascence of the human spirit which drew its vitality from currents of life which, like the Gulf Stream, were a part of the ocean of medievalism, but were changing its temperature and remaking its climate. The Reformation was not a light which "flashed directly from the clouds" with meteorlike suddenness—an unexplained effect without any discoverable cause. Rather was it the thunderous flash of a spiritual explosion, the powder of which had been accumulating for centuries and the fuse to which had been smoldering for generations.

Protestantism, therefore, though its present embodiment is a direct outgrowth of the sixteenth-century Reformation, was not born at that time. Its ancestral lineage is to be traced back through the Reformers before the Reformation—men of action such as Wycliffe, Huss, Jerome of Prague; men of thought such as John of Goch, John of Wesel, John Wessell, John Tauler, and John Staupitz; mystics such as Gerhard Groot and Thomas à Kempis; back through Augustine; back through Paul; back through Jesus; back through postexilic and exilic psalmists; back through Jeremiah and the seventh-century Hebrew prophets; back through Isaiah and the eighth-century Hebrew prophets;

179

back through the younger David; back through Moses; back to Abraham. Though recent in its present form, Protestantism is as old as vital religion. It is not a sixteenth-century aberration in the Christian tradition, a breach of Christian continuity produced by impatient, willful fanatics who broke with the past. It is rather a return to the past, "a going back to something already fixed and original . . . a deliberate return to primitive Christianity." Nor is it a mere negative protest made by dissatisfied critics of the *status quo*. Rather it is a positive quickening of the fibers of the soul which calls for the building of "more stately mansions" and thus brings it into direct conflict with the "outgrown shell" from which it seeks to free itself. But this protest against all that thwarts life and growth is not the central quality of Protestantism —it is but the converse side of a positive experience of religious vitality which gives it its essential character.

PROTESTANT AFFIRMATIONS

WINFRED ERNEST GARRISON

To avoid the tedious repetition of the phrase let it be assumed
that the words "Protestantism affirms" precede every item and
every affirmative statement that follows:

  I. *Broad Principles Held by Many Religions*
    1. The spiritual ground of all reality
    2. A moral order in the world
    3. The good life as an aspect of religion
 II. *Basic Christian Beliefs*
    1. God as Creator and Father
    2. Christ as Lord and Saviour
    3. The Church as the Body of Christ and the community
       of believers
    4. The Bible as having unique religious value
    5. The relevance of Christianity to personal and social
       morality
III. *Protestantism's Distinctive Affirmations*
    1. Justification by faith
    2. The freedom and vocation of the Christian man
    3. The priesthood of all believers
    4. The sufficiency of the Bible

The Protestant conception of the Church is one which is
consistent with justification by faith alone, the freedom of the
Christian man, the priesthood of all believers, and unrestricted
access to a Bible which, without supplementation by tradition
or interpretations dogmatically imposed by the rulers of the
Church, "containeth all things necessary to salvation."

Such a Church must of necessity be one that constitutes a genuine community and fellowship of believers, stresses the inner qualities of mind and heart rather than the performance of measured stints of meritorious ritual works, permits no priestly caste to establish a monopoly on the means of grace and no oligarchy of prelates or pontifical autocrat to lord it over God's heritage, and maintains loyalty to Christ and liberty in Christ. When Protestants exercise their freedom of inquiry and examine the basic charter upon which the Church rests, namely, the New Testament, this is the kind of Church they find that it describes.

THE CONTRIBUTION OF PROTESTANTISM

PAUL TILLICH

The most important contribution of Protestantism to the world in the past, present, and future is the principle of prophetic protest against every power which claims divine character for itself—whether it be church or state, party or leader. Obviously, it is impossible to build a church on the basis of a pure protest, and that attempt has been the mistake of Protestantism in every epoch. But the prophetic protest is necessary for every church and for every secular movement if it is to avoid disintegration. It has to be expressed in every situation as a contradiction to man's permanent attempts to give absolute validity to his own thinking and acting. And this prophetic, Protestant protest is more necessary today than at any time since the period of the Reformation, as the protest against the demonic abuse of those centralized authorities and powers which are developing under the urge of the new collectivism. It is in this Protestant protest that the eternal value of liberalism is rooted. Without this prophetic criticism the new authorities and powers will necessarily lead toward a new and more far-reaching disintegration. This criticism requires witnesses and martyrs. Without these, the prophetic and Protestant protest never has been and never will be actual.

THE EVANGELICAL HERITAGE

ANGUS DUN

Those of us who treasure the evangelical heritage believe that the Christian does not stand in intellectual or moral bondage to any man, to any hierarchy or any priesthood. He is to be constantly referred beyond the Church to the Lord of the Church and summoned to make his own responsible answer as a free man to the rightful Lord of his life. And there—to use Luther's great phrase—the freedom of the Christian man is found. We evangelicals believe that men and women who have found this freedom are the surest guardians and maintainers of a free and responsible society. It is men who know their inseparable responsibility before God, and who know that they cannot pass that responsibility on to anyone else, who are most prepared to take their responsibilities in the troubled affairs of mankind. So evangelicals are not enthusiastic when the undue exaltation of priests, or even of bishops, encourages that "flight from freedom" which is such a disturbing mark of our time . . .

There is no final guarantee in ecclesiastical correctness. So the evangelical is always concerned, beneath or beyond all the important outward ordering of the Church's life, with what is happening to persons and in persons, and between persons; between human persons and God, between human persons and Christ.

MESSAGE TO THE CHURCH

ARTHUR LICHTENBERGER

It is not enough for the Church to exhort men to be good. Men, women and children are today risking their livelihood and their lives in protesting for their rights. We must support and strengthen their protest in every way possible, rather than give support to the forces of resistance by our silence.

185

*That they all may be one; as thou,
Father, art in me, and I in thee, that
they also may be one in us: that the
world may believe that thou hast sent
me.*

Jesus Christ

That All May Be One

We have seen how Christianity and Judaism share a common source in the Old Testament; how, with the coming of Jesus, a Christian tradition was established with the New Testament as its source; and how, with the Reformation, the mainstream of Christianity became many streams, each with a tradition of its own.

But, as all streams must eventually flow to the sea, so do all these streams and their sources converge toward the great sea of truth that is all-embracing.

We are fortunate in living in a time when men in America and all over the world are beginning to realize that the faith we hold in common is more important than the traditions which may divide us. As a result, there has been a drawing together, first of denominations with similar traditions, then of Protestant churches in general, and, most recently, of Protestant, Catholic and Orthodox churches. This is called the Ecumenical Movement. The word *ecumenical* comes from the Greek, *oikoumenikos*, meaning "of or from the whole world," and it describes exactly the intention of the movement, which is to realize the words of Jesus quoted above.

Men of goodwill the world over share this dream. We hope this book will help you to understand it.

Index